T0012479

CULTURE SMART!

NEPAL

THE ESSENTIAL GUIDE TO CUSTOMS & CULTURE

TESSA FELLER
AND ALAN MERCEL-SANCA

KUPERARD

"The real voyage of discovery consists not in
seeking new landscapes, but in having new eyes."

Adapted from Marcel Proust, *Remembrance of Things Past.*

ISBN 978 1 78702 872 2

British Library Cataloguing in Publication Data
A CIP catalogue entry for this book is available
from the British Library

First published in Great Britain
by Kuperard, an imprint of Bravo Ltd
59 Hutton Grove, London N12 8DS
Tel: +44 (0) 20 8446 2440
www.culturesmart.co.uk
Inquiries: publicity@kuperard.co.uk

Design Bobby Birchall
Printed in Turkey

ABOUT THE AUTHORS

TESSA FELLER studied German and Spanish at Edinburgh University before training as a teacher and translator. She has worked in several countries, including Austria, Russia, and Germany, where she is now based. She lived in Nepal for three years when her husband was posted there with the German Development Service (Deutscher Entwicklungsdienst). Her youngest son was born in Kathmandu.

ALAN MERCEL-SANCA graduated in History at the University of Kent, and is an artist who has exhibited in New York and features in the *Best of Worldwide Charcoal, Pastel & Pencil Artists*. A frequent visitor to Nepal, he is CEO of the UK–Nepal Friendship Society, an organization that aims to protect and promote the cultures of Nepal. In 2015 he directed the UK contribution to the Nepal Art Council's Britain–Nepal Bicentenary Art Exhibition. He has led an initiative to boost the British Nepali community's participation in the UK's democratic processes by engaging the main community organizations with Parliament in Westminster.

CONTENTS

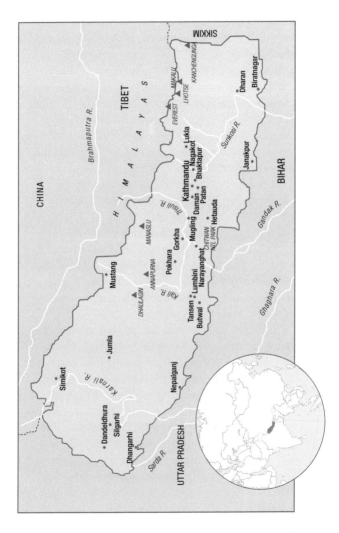

INTRODUCTION

In the popular imagination Nepal is a land of eternal snow, where heroic mountaineers and Sherpas valiantly plant flags on the roof of the world or perish in the attempt. And yet there is far more to Nepal than the ultimate challenge to mountaineers, or the peerless courage and professionalism of the Gurkhas. Nestling in the foothills of the Himalayas, it has to be one of the most diverse countries in the world, for its climate, scenery, flora, fauna, and not least on account of the great variety of its cultural, ethnic, and religious weave.

Nepal, birthplace of the Lord Buddha (at the pilgrimage site of Lumbini) possesses a vibrant spirituality that is immediately evident in different facets of daily life across the country, from the plains of the south to the high Himalayas. This aspect of its culture is deeply attractive to many Westerners who feel uncomfortable with their own dogmatic religious traditions or disenchanted with the shallow materialism of twenty-first century life.

Contrasts and incongruities abound: spectacular snow-capped peaks rise above dusty plains; the Abominable Snowman meets abominable heat; two-, three-, and four-wheeled vehicles career chaotically around an overcrowded capital, while in the mountains, nothing moves faster than a mule. There are still many social divisions today—between rich and poor, the privileged and the disempowered, urban and rural, highlands and lowlands. And yet a certain "unity in diversity" binds the country together. Hindu and Buddhist values predominate and help to maintain social harmony, and the charm and warmth of Nepal's people is underpinned by its justified reputation as one of the most important spiritual destinations.

Nepal was isolated from the rest of the world for centuries. Never a colony of a foreign Western power, its extreme terrain has both protected it from outside geo-political influence and slowed its development. Its relative inaccessibility has also allowed pockets of contrasting cultures to flourish.

Culture Smart! Nepal introduces you to this cultural, ethnic, and religious mosaic. It seeks to explain the complexities of Nepali life, from the home, to the marketplace, to the office. It describes how the country's geography and history have helped shape contemporary society, and how religion has defined its social structures and left an indelible imprint on the Nepali psyche. Today, in the age of social media and with the establishment of a secular federal republic in place of an absolute monarchy, this is beginning to change. It helps you to understand Nepali attitudes and values, giving you an idea of what to expect, and how to avoid faux pas.

You are unlikely to meet an unfriendly face in Nepal. Although in 2019 it ranked as the thirty-first poorest country in the world—which itself demonstrates a rapid advance from being among the ten poorest countries just ten years before—this will not detract from the warmth and genuineness of the welcome you will encounter. Whatever the reason for your visit, an understanding of the cultural backdrop will help you to go beyond the friendly smiles and greetings, and turn your visit into an enlightening and rewarding experience. *Namaste*!

Official Name	Federal Democratic Republic of Nepal (since May 2009)	
Capital City	Kathmandu. Pop. 1,442,000	The Kathmandu valley urban area includes the city of Patan (merged with Kathmandu) and Bhaktapur: total pop. is close to 2 million.
Main Cities	Chitwan (pop. 500,000+) and Pokhara (pop. 200,000+)	Also Patan, Biratnagar, Dharan, Bharatpur, Janakpur, Butwal
Area	56,827 square miles (147,181 sq. km)	Officially, Nepal uses the metric system. In practice, both metric and imperial are used.
Geography	Landlocked, between China (Tibet Autonomous Province) to the north and India to the south, east, and west. On a latitude with the Sahara Desert/Florida (28º00 N, 84º00 E)	
Terrain	Higher Himalayas in the far north, central hill and lower mountains region, flat river plains (the Terai) in south	
Land Use	Arable land 16.07%. Permanent crops 0.85%; other: 83.08%	Most Nepalis outside the urban areas are subsistence farmers. The best agricultural land is in the Terai/southern plains.
Climate	Alpine climate in the high mountains, temperate central valleys, subtropical southern plains	
Population	Approx. 30 million. Male 45.6% and female 54.4%	
Life Expectancy	69 for men, and for women, 72.25 (2021 estimates)	

Age Structure	0–14 years: 38.3%; 15–64 years: 57.9%; 65 years and over: 3.8%	
Literacy	67.9%: men 78.5%, women 59.7% (2021)	
Ethnic Makeup	Chhetri 15.5%, Bahun 12.5%, Magar 7%, Tharu 6.6%, Tamang 5.5%, Newar 5.4%, Muslim 4.2%, Kami 3.9%, Yadav 3.9%, other 32.7%	
Languages	Nepali 47.8%, Maithili 12.1%, Bhojpuri 7.4%, Tharu 5.8%, Tamang 5.1%, Newar 3.6%, Magar 3.3%, Awadhi 2.4%, other 12.5%. Nepali is the official language, but in higher education only English is used, and is spoken in the capital and the cities of Pokhara and Chitwan.	
Religion	Hindu 80.6%, Buddhist 10.7%, Muslim 4.2%, other 4.5%	
GDP	1,236 USD (2021). GDP growth rate is 2.7% (2021)	
Currency	Nepali Rupee (NPR), pegged to the Indian rupee. 1 USD = 118 NPR (Sept. 2021)	
Government	Federal parliamentary democracy	
Media	*Gorkhapatra* and *Kantipur* are Nepali-language dailies.	There are three government-funded state TV channels and 50+ private channels.
Media: English Language	*The Kathmandu Post, The Himalayan Times*, and *The Rising Nepal* are English-language dailies. The *Nepali Times* is a weekly. Some international periodicals are available.	
Electricity	220 volts, 50 Hz	Three-round-prong plugs used. Power supply erratic
Video/TV	PAL system	
Internet Domain	.np	
Telephone	Nepal's country code is 977.	To dial out: 00 plus country code
Time	GMT + 5 ¾ hours; EST + 10 ¾ hours	

CHAPTER ONE

LAND & PEOPLE

GEOGRAPHY

Sandwiched between China to the north, and India to the south, Nepal runs approximately 500 miles (800 km) from northwest to southeast, and is between 56 and 143 miles wide (90 and 230 km), covering an area of 56,827 square miles (147,181 sq. km). It is home not only to Mount Everest, at 29,029 feet (8,848 m) the world's highest mountain, but to eight of the ten highest peaks, and several hundred more over 20,000 feet (6,000 m).

The Himalayas give the country its unique appeal to the outside world, but this picture can be misleading: altitudes descend to less than 200 feet (60 m), and more than 40 percent of the land area is below 3,300 feet (1,000 m). The extreme variation in altitude within a small space influences everything, from Nepal's climate to its ethnicity and demography, history, and political and economic development.

More than 60 million years ago, the Indo-Australian tectonic plate collided with the Eurasian continent. The

resultant compacting of the Earth's crust over millennia, manifested through occasional earthquakes, has created a series of mountain systems running in a northwest–southeast direction. These divide Nepal into roughly parallel strips of different ecological character.

The Ganges plains extend some 25 miles (40 km) into Nepal along its southern border with India, forming the lowlands or Terai, and rising to a maximum height of 1,000 feet (300 m) above sea level. This area was infested with malaria and largely uninhabitable until sprayed with DDT in the 1950s. Now its dense forests have been cleared to make room for people from the hills, and its fertile plains, though just a fifth of the country's territory, are home to a good 50 percent of the population.

Separated from the Terai by the Mahabharat range of hills are the *pahar* (mid-hills), covering 60 percent of the

View over Phewa Lake near Pokhara with the double summit of Fishtail Mountain in the background.

land area and ranging from 1,000 feet (300 m) to nearly 15,000 feet (4,500 m) in altitude. Characteristic of these are flat, enclosed high valleys that have been inhabited for centuries, such as the highly populous and cultivated Kathmandu valley and Pokhara.

North of the mid-hills is the great Himalaya, covering almost a fifth of Nepal's territory. The few treacherous paths that traverse these high mountains, formerly trade routes between Tibet and India, are now mainly used by backpackers. The sparsely populated inner valleys of the Himalaya are screened to an extent from wind and rain, but can only be reached on foot or by airplane.

The Transhimalaya beyond is an arid desert region along the Tibetan border, in the rain shadow of the Himalayas at an average altitude of 19,700 feet (6,000 m) above sea level.

CLIMATE

There are effectively two seasons in Nepal: the dry season from October to May, and the monsoon, which starts in June and goes on until the end of September. The best times to visit are after the monsoon, in October and November, when the country is lush green and the air is clearest, and February (when the rhododendron forests are in full bloom in the countryside) through to April, before it becomes too sultry.

The Himalayas form a meteorological divide, separating the moist monsoon climate of southern Asia on one side from the arid continental climate of the Tibetan steppes on the other. The monsoon arrives from the southeast, and falls most heavily on the southern and southeastern slopes of the mountains. This is not a good time to travel, as the mountains are often obscured by clouds, and road conditions can be very poor due to mudslides and floods.

Average annual precipitation is approximately 98 inches (2,500 mm) in the east of Nepal, and 148 inches (3,755 mm) in Pokhara. Compare this with 140 inches (3,552 mm) in Seathwaite, the wettest inhabited place in England. The difference is that precipitation in England is spread evenly over twelve months, whereas in Nepal, it is concentrated into two. Rivers you can paddle in one day can turn into raging torrents overnight, sometimes washing away whole villages, roads, and bridges. Himalayan glaciers are though increasingly being impacted by global warming, making floods downstream, within Nepal and in India, more severe and unpredictable.

Terraced hills north of Kathmandu in the inner Terai.

Temperature and climate are determined by Nepal's position in the northern hemisphere (it is on a latitude with the Sahara Desert) and by altitude. While temperatures in the high mountains are permanently below freezing, temperatures in the Terai can reach 104°F (40°C) in May and June, before the monsoon breaks. The heat is compounded by high humidity. Temperatures in the capital regularly rise to 86°F (30°C) in summer, but drop pleasantly at night due to its altitude (4,265 ft/1,300 m above sea level). In January, temperatures in Kathmandu may reach 68°F (20°C) in the sun, but fall to near freezing point at night. Pokhara and especially the Terai are significantly warmer, although the Terai can feel very cold in January because blanket fog sometimes fails to lift for days at a time.

Broadly speaking, the Terai enjoys a tropical climate, the mid-hills are tropical to temperate, and the high mountains have an alpine climate. Hillsides are terraced and cultivated up to 8,900 feet (2,700 m) or the level of the clouds and mist on their southern slopes. Barley and potatoes grow to an altitude of 14,100 feet (4,300 m), which is also the tree line. The snow line, until recently, began at about 16,400 feet (5,000 m), much higher than in the Alps, but climate change is affecting this.

Climate change is a major concern. The land where the highest mountain range in the world is located has been, like the polar regions of the Arctic and Antarctic, particularly badly affected. Climatic instability is causing both the ever rising of the snow line and increasingly frequent floods and landslides, affecting human life and flora and fauna.

THE PEOPLE

Nepal, excluding the Nepali overseas diaspora, in 2019 was estimated to have a population of 29,709,449. There can be few geographical areas of similar size in this world as ethnically diverse: the census of 2001 identified ninety-two living languages, and a hundred-and-three distinct caste and ethnic groups.

Several waves of migration over two millennia brought Indo-Aryan peoples from the south together with Sino-Tibetan peoples from the north. The country's sheer topography and climatic peculiarities facilitated the preservation of separate cultural enclaves.

A demographic map of the country roughly reflects the high mountain, mid-hill, and lowland zones. Each zone can be further divided from east to west, with different ethnic groups inhabiting different regions, but the mid-hill zone is home to Bahun Chhetri, Newari, and especially the family group of Gurkha peoples spread throughout from east to west.

In the high Himalayas, Buddhist peoples of Tibetan descent predominate. These include the Sherpas in the northeast, Tamang in the Central Himalayas and hills, and Thakali further west. The Pahar (mid-hills) region is home to Rai and Limbu peoples in the east, Newars around the Kathmandu valley, and Gurung and Magar further west, as well as the originally Gorkha caste-structured Hindu Parbatiya, who include the two highest castes, Bahuns and

Chhetris, and Dalits (untouchables). Today the Parbatiya make up 40.3 percent of the total population.

Until the 1950s, the Tharu people were almost the sole inhabitants of the Terai. Today it is home to migrants from the hill areas and population overflow from the Ganges plains in India. Dominant ethnic groups are the Maithili in the east, Bhojpuri in the central Terai, and Abadhi in the west. Large numbers of Muslims from India have also settled here. About 7.3 percent of Nepalis currently live in the mountains, 44.3 percent in the central mid-hill region, and 48.4 percent in the Terai. These regions comprise 35 percent, 42 percent, and 23 percent of the total area.

A BRIEF HISTORY

Setting aside the difficulty of understanding another culture through the prism of one's own, and the real but often overlooked filter of the Western colonial narrative, there are two problems with historical accounts of Nepal. One is that most are restricted to the story of the Kathmandu valley. The second is that the history is inevitably recounted from the point of view of the dominant higher-caste Hindus (Bahuns and Chhetris).

This in itself, however, is a reflection of the country's history: the Kathmandu valley and higher-caste Hindu groups who live there have dominated politics, the economy, and Nepali society for centuries. And yet alongside them other ethnicities and people of lower castes have provided important contributions to the shaping and defining of the nation—such as the Newars (the main population of Kathmandu valley and its three cities of Kathmandu, Patan, Bhaktapur, but also found in other parts of Nepal), famous for their craftsmanship, and of course the Gurkhas, renowned for their martial prowess. At the same time, many other religious and ethnic groups contribute to the fabric of the nation.

On a geopolitical level, the combination of its topography and the fighting capability of its Gurkha population has enabled Nepal to remain independent of the dynasties and empires of the Indian lands to the south and of Tibet to the north, and to hold back the British Empire at the height of its power. Today Nepal, through the deployment of Gurkhas, makes a major contribution to global peacekeeping. Gurkhas provide the fifth-largest contingent of UN peacekeepers, and are integral components of both the British Army and the Army of India. The story of the Gurkha contribution to British influence overseas, defending the UK, and UN peacekeeping has yet to be told.

Early Inhabitants

Excavations have shown that the Kathmandu valley has been inhabited for at least 9,000 years. Both Indo-Aryan migrants from the south and Sino-Tibetan groups from the north are believed to have been present in the valley since about 1000 BCE.

The ancient Indian epics, the *Mahabharata* and *Ramayana*, provide the first documented references to the Kiratis, a Mongoloid people who dominated the valley for almost a millennium from around the eighth century BCE. The Rai and Limbu peoples of eastern Nepal are believed to be their descendants.

The Hindu kingdoms in the Terai in the first millennium BCE included the Shakya dynasty, whose most famous prince was Siddhārtha Gautama, born around 563 BCE in Lumbini, who later renounced his rank and become the founder of the Buddhist faith.

The Licchavis, 450–879

The Licchavis were Indo-Aryans who invaded from northern India around 300 CE, coming to power in the middle of the fifth century. They introduced the Hindu caste system that continues to divide society to this day, but also set a precedent for religious tolerance and syncretism. The first Licchavi king, Manadeva I, is said to have worshiped at both Hindu and Buddhist shrines.

This was a period of prosperity and cultural activity. The Buddhist temple complexes of Swayambunath and Bodhnath date from the Licchavi era, as do the Hindu temples of Changu Narayan and Pashupatinath. Mountain paths that still exist today became important trade routes linking Tibet with India. During this time, Buddhism found its way to Tibet, and one of Nepal's most important, yet today little-known, global cultural exports, the pagoda style typical of Licchavi architecture, was adopted in China and Japan.

The Thakuri Kings, 602–1200

The Thakuri kings reigned from the seventh to the thirteenth centuries, cementing their relationships with north and south by means of strategic marriages.

The daughter of Amsuvarman, the first Thakuri king, married a Tibetan prince and is said to have converted her husband to Buddhism. She is still honored today as a reincarnation of the Green Tara goddess of Tibetan Buddhism. The city of Kathmandu also dates from this era, having been founded in the tenth century. Meanwhile, the advance of Muslim conquerors in the south appears to have caused both Buddhist and Hindu clerics to take refuge in the Kathmandu valley.

The Malla Dynasty, 1200–1768

The Malla kings were a Newar dynasty that reigned in the Kathmandu valley from 1200 to 1768. The Newars today consider themselves to be the original inhabitants of the valley, but no one really knows where they came from.

After more than a century of feudal conflict, and a devastating invasion by Muslim Mughals in 1349, King Jayasthiti Malla succeeded in uniting the whole valley in 1382. He sought to impose order by implementing the rules of orthodox Hinduism. The caste system was extended to include the Buddhist Newars.

Buddhist priests took the highest social rank, like their Hindu (*Bahun*) counterparts, followed by noblemen, officials, shopkeepers, and farmers. Monks were permitted to marry and the status of priests also became hereditary, thus reinforcing their status within the social hierarchy. Priests began to perform more worldly jobs and carry out their priestly duties as secondary occupations. The tantric form of Buddhism began to spread (see Chapter 3). Newar, a Tibeto-Burmese language distinct from Tibetan and Nepali, became the language of state.

King Yaksha Malla, grandson of Jayasthiti, pursued an expansionist policy until the country extended from the Ganges in the south to Tibet in the north, and from the Kali Gandaki River in the west to Sikkim. On his death in 1482, the kingdom split into three rival kingdoms ruled from Bhaktapur, Kathmandu, and Patan.

Political feuding continued for the next two centuries, eventually inviting disaster, but culturally this period was a golden age, in which the three kingdoms vied to outdo each other in terms of architecture and art. Many of the buildings and works of art still to be admired today in Bhaktapur, Patan, and Kathmandu date from this era.

The Shah Kings and the Unification of Nepal, 1768–1846

Under the Hindu Shah dynasty, the tiny kingdom of Gorkha, some 62 miles (100 km) to the west, had been growing in strength. Although both Muslim and British troops rushed to help the Mallas, Prithvi Narayan Shah of Gorkha defeated them and unified Nepal in 1768.

Fearing European intervention, the new ruler expelled all Christian missionaries, by now associated with encroaching Western colonization, and refused entry to foreigners. Nepal entered a (first) period of self-imposed isolation—in retrospect perhaps a blessing, as the country was to be spared ever being ruled by foreigners.

In their thirst for new land, the Shah kings spread throughout the mid-hills of Nepal, bringing with them both their religion and their Nepali language, a language of Indo-Aryan origin. For a while the country extended from Kashmir in the west to Sikkim in the east.

The Chinese put a stop to their expansion when they attempted to conquer Tibet.

War Against the British, 1814–16

Meanwhile the influence of the British on the Indian subcontinent was growing. In 1814, a border dispute with the British East India Company led to war.

Nepal held the agents of the world's greatest global power at bay for two years before starting to lose territory, and long before the prospect of immediate defeat it sought an armistice. This led to the Treaty of Sugauli of 1816, by which it was forced to give up Sikkim and much of the Terai to the Company, and to tolerate a British Resident in Kathmandu, stationed there to monitor the situation. The treaty established Nepal's present-day borders, but would also burnish the country's reputation through the performance of the Gurkhas against the British forces. A further long period of isolation began. The British Residents were to be the only foreigners allowed into the country for more than a century.

The Gurkhas

The British were so impressed by the valor and tenacity of these mountain warriors, that they not only allowed them to surrender honorably with their arms, but began to employ them in the ranks of the East India Company's army. When they later proved their loyalty during the Indian Mutiny of 1857, the British Army created its elite Gurkha regiments. Since then they have become one of Nepal's most famous exports, serving not only in the British but also in the Indian Army, and in particular providing a major contribution to the work of United Nations peace-keeping. Their courage is legendary, defined by the motto of "death before dishonor," and Gurkhas have served in the British Army in both world wars, the Falklands, and Iraq. In return for their help during the two world wars, before Britain withdrew from the subcontinent Nepal was once again assured of its independence, and guaranteed duty-free transit of commodities through India.

The Ranas, 1846–1951

In 1846, Jung Bahadur Rana, a nephew of the king, had many of the most important people in the country massacred in the Kot courtyard next to Kathmandu's

The power behind the throne. Prime Minister Chandra S.J.B. Rana and his eight sons in the 1920s

Durbar Square, before declaring himself prime minister. Thereafter power was in the hands of the Rana family, who became hereditary prime ministers. The Shahs were relegated to the role of puppet kings with little more than a ceremonial function. The Ranas maintained cordial relations with Britain, rushing to help the British during the Indian Mutiny in 1857 with 8,000 Gurkhas, although the country remained isolated from the outside world.

The Hinduization of Nepal

The dominance of the Hindu ruling elite became firmly established during the Shah and Rana eras. Having unified Nepal, the ruling Parbatiya Hindus needed to consolidate their political control. They also wanted to raise revenue quickly from the conquered kingdoms in order to be able to continue expansion. Officers were rewarded with *jagirs*—gifts of conquered land.

At the same time, peace had priority over conformity. The complete subordination of so many tiny kingdoms of such varied ethnic and religious backgrounds would have been difficult. The caste system, officially codified for the first time in Jung Bahadur Rana's *Muluki Ain* (civil code) of 1854, was to give them the legal and social structure they needed to integrate the many different ethnic communities into a coherent unit.

By prescribing caste status for all groups according to how closely they adhered to Hindu norms, the code put pressure on non-Hindus to conform to Hindu standards. Groups that consumed alcohol or pork were for example lower caste than most high-caste Hindus. The *Muluki Ain* also dealt with subjects as varied as land tenure, inheritance, marriage, and sexual relations. It banned certain practices, such as the consumption of beef. It established the Hindu culture and way of thinking as the basis of the state and law, although it was neutral on the subject of other religions.

Different ethnic groups responded in different ways to Hindu dominance. Some, such as the Magars and Thakalis, sought to integrate and adopted Hindu customs. Others resisted. Many Limbus thus left for Sikkim and Darjeeling. The remoteness of other communities, such as the Sherpas, allowed them to ignore what was going on elsewhere. The recruitment of large numbers of soldiers from different ethnic groups into the British and Indian armies helped spread Parbatiya culture, however, as Nepali became the common language within the Gurkha regiments. It can be said that while the Tibeto-Burmese peoples have given the country its cultural diversity, the Indo-Aryans provide the links that hold the country together.

Other significant reforms introduced during the Ranas' rule included the banning of the practice of *suttee* (burning widows on their husbands' funeral pyres), and the abolition of slavery in 1924.

The Beginnings of Democracy
India's independence in 1947 and the Chinese annexation of Tibet in 1951 meant that Nepal became a buffer zone between the two powers. The success of India's independence movement led to calls within Nepal to end the autocratic rule of the Ranas. In 1947, the Nepali National Congress was established as the first

people's representative body. Known after 1950 as the Nepali Congress Party, it was increasingly supported by many Nepalis, including members of the royal family, and by India, which feared weak Rana rule.

In 1950, King Tribhuvan was forced to flee to India because of his support for the Nepali National Congress. His infant son was briefly proclaimed king by the Ranas, a move that provoked a short civil war. Tribhuvan returned to Kathmandu in 1951 with the support of Nehru to set up a new government under a non-Rana prime minister. King Mahendra succeeded his father in 1955, and in 1959 Nepal held its first general election. By December 1960, however, the king had declared the failure of democracy. He returned to an authoritarian style of government, banning political parties and introducing the party-less Panchayat system of government.

The Panchayat System, 1962–90

To all appearances, the Panchayat system introduced in 1962 allowed people to choose their own representatives. It involved a pyramid-like structure of Panchayat (councils) elected at the local level. Local councils then elected representatives for district councils, which in turn appointed representatives to parliament. At the top of the pyramid sat the king, however, who retained absolute authority over the prime minister and parliament. The royal family thus maintained its control of politics and the economy, while the army and police were given a free hand to suppress dissent. The media were strictly censored, and many of the leaders of the

Nepali Congress Party spent extended periods in jail during this time. Corruption was rife, and although it is impossible to prove, much government spending and foreign aid evaporated long before it reached the grass roots.

There were some achievements. Government programs built schools, increased literacy, and sought to improve communications as a means of development. Roads were built, especially with Indian investment. In an effort to develop one common culture, the Panchayat promoted Nepali as the national language and sole language of education. This policy further consolidated the dominance of the high-caste, Nepali-speaking elite, putting ethnic minorities at a disadvantage.

King Birendra and the Constitutional Monarchy, 1990–2001

In 1979, riots erupted in Kathmandu to protest the slow pace of development and perceived corruption. King Birendra, who had taken over on the death of his father, Mahendra, in 1972, offered his people the choice between a reformed Panchayat and a multiparty system. The Panchayat won by a narrow margin, and thus survived for a further decade. However, support for a multiparty system was growing, and increasing democratization was the consequence.

In 1989 an Indian blockade exacerbated a difficult economic situation in the country. The Nepali Congress called a mass demonstration in February 1990, demanding an end to the Panchayat and Indian dominance. The arrests of its leaders were followed by general strikes and further protests, which were initially suppressed brutally. The king preempted an escalation of the violence, however, by announcing the dissolution of the Panchayat and introducing a multiparty system. A new constitution emphasized the sovereignty of the people and established adult franchise, a two-house parliamentary system, a constitutional monarchy, multiparty democracy, and an independent judiciary. In May 1991, free elections were held.

Once in power, the leaders of the people's movement did not have a coherent agenda, and the first decade of democracy was characterized by political instability. Democracy brought a degree of political awareness, but few economic or social changes. The definition of the Hindu state was retained. The constitution of 1990 emphasized people's participation, but made no provision for local government. This led to a centralized structure and left a huge gulf between urban Nepal and the hill districts.

The Maoist Insurgency, 1996–2006

Various Communist groups participated actively in the people's movement of 1989–90. The Communist Party of Nepal (United Marxist-Leninist) became the second-biggest political party in the elections of 1991, and remains a mainstream political party representing the left. The CPN (Maoist) is a breakaway group formed in 1995 after numerous splits in the movement. It had never been satisfied with the constitutional monarchy and demanded the creation of a people's republic.

Disenchanted with the constant political infighting, the CPN denounced the other Communist groups for participating in the parliamentary process, and launched a People's War in 1996, with attacks on police stations in the western and mid-western regions. Brutal and indiscriminate police retaliation resulted in the almost complete alienation of the rural population. By 2001 at least forty-five out of a total of seventy-five districts were classified as "highly affected" by the insurgency.

THE ROYAL MASSACRE

On June 1, 2001, ten members of the royal family were shot dead in the royal palace. A stunned Nepali public refused to believe the official story, that in a drug-crazed frenzy, after being refused permission to marry the woman of his choice, Crown Prince Dipendra had killed nine of his closest relatives before turning the gun on himself. Rumors still abound as to the real nature of the event, ranging from a Maoist plot, to an attempted coup by foreign intelligence agencies, to a conspiracy organized by the new king.

When a brief cease-fire in 2001 permitted talks the Maoists took the opportunity to seek a new constitution, arguing that after the massacre, "the traditional monarchy based on feudal nationalism has ended."

On November 26, 2001, the government responded to the resumption of attacks on police and military installations in the western hills by declaring a state of emergency, mobilizing the army for the first time. Taking advantage of the post-9/11 world political climate, they also declared the Maoists to be terrorists. Whereas the first six years of the civil war had cost three thousand lives, an estimated seven thousand people were killed in the first year of the army's involvement. Human rights abuses were cimmitted by both sides.

By late 2002 the insurgents controlled seven of seventy-five districts, mainly in the mid-west. In these areas, they set up people's governments and courts, levied taxes, organized development programs, and controlled basic health and education services. They then began to use terror to expand into other areas, murdering or threatening local leaders to send them into flight to create power vacuums, blocking roads and bridges to isolate regions, forcibly recruiting, and generally intimidating the population. Rural people were often caught in a no-win situation, coerced into feeding the Maoists by night, and punished for doing so by the Royal Nepal Army by day.

As it seemed unlikely in May 2002 that Prime Minister Deuba's government would obtain the majority it needed to extend the state of emergency, he asked King Gyanendra to dissolve the House of Representatives and call elections. In order to prevent the Maoists influencing the elections through intimidation, Deuba then simply replaced existing, elected local committees with government officials. Democratic structures were thus removed at both national and local levels.

When it then appeared that it would be impossible to organize any elections for as long as the Maoist conflict lasted, Deuba asked the king to postpone them indefinitely. Gyanendra seized the opportunity to restore the absolute power of the monarchy. He dismissed the government on October 4, 2002, and proceeded to appoint a series of governments himself. Their mandate was to end the insurgency and organize parliamentary elections. This was made impossible by the Maoists, and by the Royal Nepal Army, who refused to take orders from anyone but the king.

The Royal Putsch of February 2005

Citing the continued political disarray and inability of the political parties to contain the insurgency, on February 1, 2005, King Gyanendra sacked the government again, declared a state of emergency, and assumed direct rule himself. It amounted to a royal putsch, not because he had dissolved parliament, given that the latter was illegitimate anyway, but because at the same time he suspended many fundamental human rights. Many politicians, journalists, human rights activists, students, and intellectuals were arrested, and the state assumed control over all media. Immediately after the broadcasting of Gyanendra's "putsch speech," all telecommunication systems were switched off. The country was cut off from the outside world.

But the king had miscalculated. By depriving people of their rights he turned both political parties and civil society into opponents of the monarchy. His actions finally caused the Maoist rebels and political parties to unite against him. Pro-democracy demonstrations became increasingly anti-monarchy.

Despite day-time curfews, demonstration bans, and violent clampdowns by the security forces, a nineteen-day protest organized by the seven-party alliance and civil society with the tacit support of the Maoists in April 2006 drew unprecedented numbers of demonstrators representing all sectors of society throughout the country. On April 24 the king backed down and reinstated the parliament he had dissolved in 2002.

A parliamentary resolution stripped the king of his powers and privileges, established an interim government, and officially secularized what had been the only Hindu state in the world. On November 21, 2006, a declaration of peace ended the ten-year insurgency that, according to UN figures, had left 13,000 people dead, and 100,000 displaced. Against this grim backdrop the scene was at last set for the first tentative steps toward the creation of a new Nepal worthy of all sections and sub-population groups of the nation.

NEPAL TODAY

Federal Republic

In 2007 an Interim Constitution was drawn up, to be reviewed and ratified at a later date, and in 2008 the monarchy was formally abolished. In May that year Nepal became a federal, democratic republic, and in August the republic's first government was formed by Pushpa Kamal Dahal, known as "Prachanda" ("Fierce"!).

Subsequently, for almost a decade, Nepal experienced a succession of often short-lived governments.

The Constitution of September 2015, which superseded the Interim Constitution, has 308 Articles, 9 Schedules, and 35 parts. Nepal became a federal republic with seven provinces replacing the fourteen former administrative zones. Executive power in each province is vested in a council of ministers and a governor, who is appointed by the president of the Federal Democratic Republic. The chief minister/governor is the leader of the party with a majority in the provincial assembly.

The existing village development committees (VDCs) were dissolved in March 2017 and replaced by 460 Gaunpalikas (rural municipalities), which are the new lower administrative unit in Nepal.

In Article 4 of the Constitution Nepal was defined as an "independent, indivisible, sovereign, Hindu, inclusive, democratic, socialism-oriented, federal, democratic republican state." The restructuring of Nepal into a federal republic has gone far to address the need for regional and local autonomy in this ethnically diverse nation. The bicameral parliamentary system consists of two federal houses, and unicameral parliaments in each of the newly constituted seven provinces. At national level, a mixed electoral system—combining proportional representation with first-past-the-post—was adopted for the elections to the lower federal house.

Human Rights, and Wrongs

The new Constitution enshrines inclusiveness, human rights, and women's rights (significantly it is largely written in gender-neutral terms), and protects gender and sexual minorities.

While mindful of the need to preserve Nepal's record of freedom from religious strife and its thriving, inclusive religious environment, the Constitution also contains an article prohibiting proselytization—active approaches to others in order to convert them to a religion not their own by birth or choice. This provision was prompted by seeing the toxic effects of proselytization—social disruption and often deadly conflict—in other lands.

Since unification in 1768, Nepal has been multiethnic, multilingual, multicultural, and multireligious, and has never lost its independence. Nevertheless, many feel that historically only a small minority ever profited from this development. Today, the expansion of education at all ages and levels, and widespread engagement in the democratic process, with the attendant idea of rights and responsibilities, have brought the voices and the issues of underprivileged groups increasingly to the fore.

The new, democratic Nepal has fostered ethnic inclusion and non-discrimination. Ethnic unrest that had erupted before in the Terai reoccurred in 2015. The aggrieved Madhesi—who are ethnically close to the Indian Biharis and who have a history of perceived exclusion and discrimination—felt that at this crucial time the hill-dominated elites, now including the Maoists, were denying them a fair share in power.

India's support for the Madhesi made the situation incendiary, with an undeclared but de-facto economic blockade, including fuel (at that time there was still an almost 100 percent dependency on India for the importation of petroleum), for much of 2015. This was aggravated by the fact that the blockade was imposed very soon after the disastrous earthquakes that hit Nepal that year, and amid suspicions of subversive activity by India, particularly through political actors in the neighboring Indian province of Bihar. Despite great passions on both sides, the situation was defused, in a major test for the new Nepal; in 2019 one of the two deputy prime ministers held his post on behalf of a Madhesi political party that was part of the government.

Nepal in 2019 was in the unique position of being led by a majority government composed by the fusion of two of the three main national political parties, with common perspectives on national values and priorities. This is something that rarely happens in poltics, and was in marked contrast to many other countries, including some "mature" democracies in the West.

The Nepali government is reaching out to current and potentially new future friendly nations overseas for development investment. Its approach is Trade not Aid. In other words, it is looking for constructive, practical support and mutually respectful relations at a bilateral level. Outdated attitudes such as "Nepal is a Third World country that can't help itself and can only be supported by First World Aid" are no longer appropriate.

THE ECONOMY

Nepal's urban population has jumped from 9 percent in 2008 to 20 percent in 2019, especially evident in the

Rice planting in the paddy fields of Ramechhap District.

phenomenal growth of the Kathmandu valley metropolis in the past ten years. It is still, however, largely an agrarian nation, although this is changing, with the rise in its urban population often being matched by marked depopulation in remote areas such as the far west.

Population pressure and the Maoist conflict led to migration from the countryside to the towns, and from the hill regions to the Terai, but industrial development has not been able to provide jobs for all. There is still a considerable shortage of skilled labor, further exacerbated by workers seeking economic opportunities abroad, mainly in India, the Gulf states, and Malaysia. Nepal's largest source of foreign currency, more than it receives from exports, aid, and tourism put together, comes in the form of remittances from people working abroad. However, it is expected that this drain of human resources will slow down as opportunities are created at home. Politicians of all parties are increasingly committed to the development of employment and wealth creation opportunities in Nepal, which is essential to the goal of achieving Developed Nation Status by 2032. Moreover, reports of the appalling conditions of manual labor in some of the Gulf countries in particular reveal instances of virtual slavery and often fatalities due to poor safety on building sites. Nepalis are concerned by such grim realities.

Tourism is the country's most important industry. Improvement of standards and diversification have been taking place at an accelerated pace since the mid-2010s, and there has been a strong recovery of the sector since the April 2015 earthquake. Traditional cottage industries feed the tourist industry with handicrafts and, beyond the purchases of artwork and items of clothing, Nepali culture, festivals, and high-quality traditional food are among some of the attractions for tourists.

Manufacturing is mostly concentrated in the Kathmandu valley and the Terai. In the absence of natural resources of any significance, it consists mainly of the processing of imported raw materials or of local agricultural produce such as grain, jute, tobacco, and sugar cane. There are also cement and brick factories, soft drinks plants (American investors), and chemical factories (Indian investors). The main exports are vegetable ghee, clothing, carpets, leather goods, jute goods, and grain. More than half of all exports go to

India. The USA (garments) and Germany (carpets) are its second- and third-biggest export partners.

However, the development of Nepal's phenomenal potential in hydropower is increasingly shaping plans for growth and diversification of the economy. Moreover, the problem of electricity "load-shedding" that characterized the first half of the decade has been largely overcome by the Nepal Electricity Authority; without this great accomplishment economic growth, dependent on a steady uninterrupted power supply, would simply not have been possible.

It is also being seen as important to retain the major human resources Nepal possesses in a number of areas—tailoring, clothing, fashion creation, and design, which other countries' economies have been benefiting from—within the country for the benefit of Nepal itself.

COVID-19

Nepal responded swiftly to the coronavirus pandemic in early 2020, closing air and land borders, particularly with China and India, and imposing strict containment measures, including quarantine and rigorous testing. Lives were saved, but the economic cost of these public health measures was substantial. There was a complete lockdown of the vital tourism sector; remittances from overseas Nepali workers fell dramatically as jobs were lost around the world; and the restrictions halted the post-2015 earthquake reconstruction work, which had been generating jobs and income in very many localities.

CHAPTER TWO

VALUES &
ATTITUDES

It is difficult to generalize about values and attitudes in Nepal because of the sheer diversity of its communities, the disparity between rich and poor, and the gulf in experience, education, and opportunity between urban and rural dwellers. The Nepali attitude to life, compared, for example, to that in Western countries, is still largely religious and spiritual, and highly civic, with a strong sense of social responsibility. Social attitudes are characterized by both a clear awareness of authority and social structure on the one hand, and humane and inclusive activities on the other.

CIVIC SPIRIT AND COMMUNITY AND SOCIAL ACTION

Visitors to Nepal will, if they engage with Nepalis beyond the usual tourist and tours contexts, find to their delight, and often to their surprise, that Nepalis, especially those in higher education and in their twenties and thirties, possess a refreshing dynamism.

The younger generation of leaders of the new Nepal combine respectful sensitivity to traditional values with practical, often cutting-edge, solutions to pressing social and economic problems. They have in common a contemporary "one nation" vision of social inclusion and democratic needs.

Coupled with this is the phenomenon of the newly created local councils and development committees, which seek to assist both local citizens and society as a whole at a grassroots community level. The traditional social and community ethic is carried forward by the younger generation in other social settings and is a decisive influence in contemporary Nepal. This pragmatic yet culturally sensitive approach is auspicious for Nepal's future. Indeed, it is very rare not to find business community leaders and professionals not also engaging in major social and community support activity of one kind or another.

KARMA, DHARMA—FATALISM OR A SPUR TO ACTION

Karma and *Dharma* are both Hindu and Buddhist concepts. Through the concept of *Karma* they offer an explanation for the apparently random variety of individual human circumstances.

Hindus believe in reincarnation and *karma*, which in Sanskrit means Action, or Deed. The way we lead our current lives has consequences for our status not only in future lives, but for the present. If our situation is bad, it may be because of something we have done in a past life, and if good, due to actions and decisions made in past lives. Success is good *karma* (a reward) and failure is bad *karma* (a punishment), and what matters are our decisions in the here and now, which determine which of these we bring about. Because *Karma* is a spiritual concept, the motivation of the actions we take and the words we choose to use should be pure. We have the choice to do the right thing for our character development, often linked to helping our fellow human beings, especially those in states of suffering.

In real terms, belief in *karma* has led to both activism and passivity. On the one hand, those who subscribe to *karma* can be passive and fatalistic in the face of adversity, or fail to take ethical decisions, which can, for example lead, to a shrugging of shoulders in the face of difficult situations. On the other hand, it can inspire heroic self-sacrifice and courageous deeds delivered at great personal cost.

Dharma is the obligation to accept one's condition in life and perform the duties associated with it conscientiously. The poor must fulfil their *dharma* without envy. The rich must fulfil theirs without self-criticism but with a sense of humility and the imperative to use their good *karma* to generate still more good *karma* by thinking of those less fortunate than themselves and contributing to the betterment of society—the reverse of this being a squandering of good *karma*. So we see that there can be on the one hand a disempowering fatalism on the part of those who accept *karma* and *dharma* at face value, without reflection on the teachings underlying both—for example, the mistaken idea that there is no shame attached to begging, because it's *karma*—and on the other, a powerful incentive to take action, as seen in Nepal in the phenomenon of social works and initiatives undertaken for personal well-being or that of the broader community.

THE CASTE SYSTEM

Authority and social status in Nepal are dictated by the caste system, which exists for most but not all ethnic groups, but particularly those who follow Hinduism. Officially abolished in 1963, in practice caste remains fundamental to people's understanding of the society in which they live, affecting politics, business, and social relations. It still influences who gets which job, who studies where, and who associates with whom. However, it is essential not to see caste as a social classification that all Nepalis accept unthinkingly.

There is a major difference in attitudes toward caste between Hindus and Buddhists. The Buddha severely criticized the caste system. In his view and in that of Buddhism caste may be used as an excuse for not taking the necessary actions to realize Enlightenment. Hence perhaps his famous saying: "Birth does not make one a priest or an outcaste. Behavior makes one either a priest or an outcaste."

THE CASTES

The *Muluki Ain* of 1854 codified the caste system in Nepal by putting social groups into five broad categories according to how closely they adhered to Hindu norms:

1. Wearers of the holy thread: Bahuns, Chhetris, Rajputs, and various Newar castes
2. Non-enslavable *matawali* (alcohol drinkers): Magar, Gurung, some Newar
3. Enslavable *matawali*: Limbu, Kirat, Tharu, Bhote (the latter includes Sherpas, Tamang, and others)
4. Impure but touchable: Newar service castes, butchers, washermen, tanners, and Europeans and Muslims
5. Impure and untouchable (Dalits): Parbatiya (blacksmiths, tanners, tailors) and Newar service castes (fishermen and scavengers)

The *matawali* of categories 2 and 3, apart from the Newars, incorporate the ethnic groups that had been outside the caste system prior to 1854. They were non-enslavable or enslavable presumably according to power play among the different groups at the time. Thus Gurungs could not be sold, whereas Tamang could.

The system has never been as rigid as the caste system in India, and some minorities in remote areas simply ignore it. Nevertheless, the caste system gives information about possible occupations and working activities, eating habits, and behavior. Only the highest caste, Bahuns, may be priests. Many of them are vegetarian, as eating meat would make them impure. At the other end of the scale, any job involving the killing or processing of animals is low in status (fishermen, butchers, leather workers, drum makers).

Those following traditional norms believe that physical contact with lower castes will sully the purity of high castes. A high-caste person will not eat with a low-caste person, or accept water from him, although he may help himself. Intercaste marriage is still unusual, and there is very little mixing between castes socially.

The 2015 Constitution, the age of the Internet, and the "global village," are however factors that are increasingly challenging the credibility and perpetuation of the caste system. There is, for example, a real and growing defiance of the status quo as unethical and moribund in cases of arranged family marriages or of love between two individuals that challenges the norm.

The "Pork Eater"

It took us several days on a trek to work out why one of our four porter-guides, although keen to explain details of mountain scenery to us or build "campfires" with our children, refused to accept our invitation to join us for meals. When we asked, it had nothing to do with us: the other three guides, all Bahun or Chhetri, would not permit a Gurung "pork eater" to eat with them.

Members of higher castes may assume certain privileges, such as expecting instant service in a shop. Some caste groups can be recognized by other Nepalis by the way they dress. Many surnames also immediately tell those in the know something about the caste background of those they are dealing with. It takes a long time for Westerners to become attuned to caste distinctions, but castes play an important role in Nepali society.

In Nepali Tantric Buddhism there is a separate caste for priests, with those from other castes not being allowed to join the priesthood.

THE IMPORTANCE OF THE FAMILY

The family is the most important social unit in Nepal. Families tend to be larger, especially in rural areas, and more extended than Western families. Older members of the family are much respected by younger generations, and expect to be looked after by their sons in old age. There is a clear family hierarchy, with greatest respect reserved for the patriarch—in most cases the father, otherwise the eldest son/brother. Several generations may live under one roof. When a son marries, his wife will normally move into his parental home, where she is answerable to her mother-in-law as well as her husband. It is unusual for a young couple to set up on their own, ut this is changing.

It is extremely important for Nepalis to have children. Apart from meaning security in old age, sons in particular are of great religious significance, as they prepare their parents for the next life during special cremation rites. Childlessness is still commonly an unquestioned reason for divorce, and the eldest son is always expected to marry.

People derive strength from their family, and also bear responsibility toward it. The head of the family is ultimately responsible for the others, making all important decisions and arranging marriage partners and sometimes jobs for family members. In return the patriarch expects respect and loyalty. What we in the West might see as blatant nepotism or even exploitation is regarded in Nepal as the familial responsibility of better-placed family members toward their relatives.

In Nepal same-sex couples or families are rare, though numbers are growing. There is still extensive cultural resistance and social hostility toward homosexuality, and same-sex marriage is illegal. Thus gay people have to conceal their relationships due to fear of family, friends, employers' enmity, rejection, and persecution; the age-old custom in South Asia of couples having marriages of convenience with members of the opposite sex (often fellow LGB community members) still continues.

THE *APHNO MANCHE* CONCEPT— A FAMILY SUPPORT GROUP

Nepalis will try to organize things through family members or through a select circle of people whom they know and can call upon. These may be friends, although the relationship is not always an equal one. It is reciprocal in the sense that it is based on mutual trust and respect. Benevolence and patronage are essentially offered in return for obedience and loyalty. Each of the two parties thinks of the other as an *aphno manche* ("own person").

To give an example, one family may lend money to another to build a house. In return, members of the debtor family can be called upon to do various jobs, such as helping slaughter a goat, or with heavy digging in the garden. Or a young man might be lent money to allow him to travel to the Middle East to work on building sites. In return, his younger brother may go to work for the lender as a servant. If he works hard and is obedient, he may be found a job later as an adult, so that the relationship between patron and beneficiary continues. Where we might see this as exploitation, the lender will probably consider his action to be philanthropy.

In public life, political affiliation plays a role in *aphno manche* loyalties.

THE *JAGIR* CULTURE

Closely related to the *aphno manche* phenomenon is the "*jagir* culture," a contemporary form of feudal relationship originating with the Shahs, based on the Indian Mughal regimes of the sixteenth and seventeenth centuries, and successively consolidated under the Ranas and the Panchayat. Its key features are preserved in Nepal's state machinery and political organizations today.

Historically, deserving vassals were rewarded by the ruler with a temporary land tenancy known as a *jagir*.

The responsibilities of the *jagirdar* (official) were to raise an army in the event of war (that is, show loyalty, be the ruler's *aphno manche*) and to make a contribution to the treasury. Otherwise, the *jagirdar* was absolute ruler over his fiefdom, playing the roles of judge, tax collector, and governor.

The ministries and state organizations are today's *jagirs*. Personal connections are the key to recruitment. For selection into key ministries, a "premium" may be required. The highest premiums are exacted by the Ministries of Finance (taxes), Commerce (imports), and Forestry. Those ministries with access to foreign aid and grants are the most lucrative and thus most prestigious.

Promotions are made on the basis of points gained for seniority, years of service, and education. There are no points for a job well done. Productivity, innovation, and hard work are thus all suppressed by this system: a premium or the right connections are what may swing the balance.

Typical of this culture is the idea, "A government employee (*jagirdar*) is not a public servant, the public serves him." Another management saying is that "The work that gets done is the work that is rewarded." In the case of a District Forest Officer, this means cutting down trees rather than planting them; in the case of the tax official, it means harassing businessmen into "making a donation."

A government employee would lose face if he were not able to extend favors such as jobs to his political supporters or family. Temporary positions may be created even where there is no work. Officials are not held accountable and so have little sense of responsibility.

As civil servants are rotated in their positions every two years in Nepal—ironically enough, to prevent corruption—there is no continuity. The effect is devastating, since it prevents people from developing a vision for the future, or initiating and implementing change. In a worst-case scenario, officials have two years to make good the premium they paid in the first place!

In the current age of the Federal Democratic Republic of Nepal, with Nepal's commitment to work toward achieving Developed Nation status by 2032, this time-honored system is likely to be challenged, as the successful delivery of specific performance goals depends on the harnessing of merit and ability.

RESPECT

Respect is a key value in Nepal. It is mutual respect that has allowed the multitude of different cultural, ethnic, and religious groups to coexist peacefully for centuries. Perhaps the most important form of respect is the tradition of respect for one's elders. Age is not a cause of embarrassment in Nepal, but a requirement for respect. This is reflected in forms of address used to speak even to complete strangers. If you are perceived to be older than the person addressing you, they will call you *Didi*, meaning "older sister," or *Dai* ("older brother"); if you are perceived to be younger *Bhai* (for men) and *Bahini* (for women) are used to signify "younger brother" or "younger sister." You may also be addressed as "Uncle" or "Auntie." These are entirely respectful terms. Similarly, a *-jee* (also

-*ji*) suffix added to someone's name when you address them is a mark of respect. It may be attached to a first name ("John-*jee*") or to a surname ("Brown-*jee*"). The suffix -*jiu* is used for very senior respected figures such as ministers, prime ministers, organization leaders, experts, ambassadors, and so on.

Caste status, wealth, and success also command respect. Someone who is wealthy and successful is a *thulo manche* ("great/important person"—literally "Great Man"). It is not necessarily important how the wealth or success has been created.

Contradictory attributes may draw respect. Wealth is respected, and yet so is self-denial and humility. This is seen in the respect shown to penniless *sadhus* (wise men and ascetics) who wander from house to house seeking alms.

MAINTAINING FACE

Tied in with notions of respect is the importance of maintaining face. Nepalis do not like to criticize, contradict, or disagree with a person directly, because this would cause them to lose face. Nor do they like to admit to not understanding something, as they hemselves then lose face.

They rarely say "No" directly. An evasive answer may well be an attempt to make "No" more palatable. Be prepared for ambiguity and aware that people may tell you what they think you want to hear. This can be particularly the case on culturally sensitive subjects (such as caste) so it is best to avoid these and self-check on making any statements that imply Nepali culture has any defects, or that Western perspectives might be right and superior.

TRADITION AND SUPERSTITION

Nepalis set great store by tradition. Many traditions are respected in an almost superstitious belief that doing things according to tradition will bode well for the future. The date for a wedding is traditionally always fixed by a priest and according to astrology. Most traditions are religious; some are to do with rites of passage. Some of the most important are described later.

ATTITUDES TOWARD WORK AND KEEPING UP APPEARANCES

Caste status and a person's level of success determine what work or activities he or she is likely to be willing to participate in. It no longer befits the status of someone who has earned a degree to perform manual work or get himself dirty, except perhaps in a recreational, family, and informal setting. Traditional norms of interaction with others mean that, for example, the boss commands respect, even if he is not actually seen to do very much all day. It befits his status to delegate to other people. A successful, wealthy man is unlikely to wind down on the weekend by doing a bit of gardening—he would lose standing by doing so. Nor is he likely to be a DIY enthusiast.

This attitude is why you will occasionally see people with one or more particularly long fingernail. These are a status symbol, showing that the person does not have to work with his hands. Office jobs in towns are the jobs of choice. Government employees such as doctors or teachers sent to work in remote areas consequently often fail to turn up, although such behavior is increasingly being rejected as unacceptable.

Nepalese women like to show their status by donning fine clothes and jewellery when they go out. Traditionally they own only the jewelry given to them by their husbands. The more gold they wear, the wealthier their husband.

Traditional ideas of beauty mean that the tall, sticklike cover girls of the Western world have little allure for most Nepali men. A few extra pounds in weight are a sign of wealth, and the adjectives *moto* (for men), meaning "well-fleshed," and *moti* (for women) are entirely positive.

ATTITUDES TOWARD WOMEN

In some Nepali sub-cultures women enjoy a high status. Generally, however, Nepali women have traditionally been disadvantaged both legally and socially. The law has only recently changed to allow a woman not married by the age of thirty-five to inherit an equal share from her parents. Her dowry is otherwise her share, and as this constitutes a considerable expense to her family, the birth of a boy is preferred. However, there are sometimes, rarely, instances of dowries being put

Newar woman carrying water containers.

to exceptional use by wives with the support of their husbands, such as, in the case of Sabita Uppreti, being used for altruistic purposes such as setting up schools and centers for children with disabilities. The September 2015 Constitution explicitly recognizes the rights of women with a provision stating that "women shall have equal ancestral right without any gender-based discrimination."

Gender determination clinics exist, and female feticide is undoubtedly an issue. Women suspected of having an abortion may be imprisoned. Girl trafficking to brothels in India and beyond is still a very real problem, with Nepali children's and women's rights organizations undertaking exceptional work to reduce this.

According to a Nepali saying, "Having a daughter is like planting a seed in another man's garden." Girls officially change families upon marriage. They enter their husband's family at the lowest level, gaining in status only when they produce a child, preferably a son. Traditionally they are expected to defer to their husbands and in-laws at all times. Daughters do, however, maintain a special relationship with their *maiti* (maternal home), and when permitted to visit after marriage, they are likely to be treated there as princesses, higher in status than their sisters-in-law.

Menstruating women or those who have just given birth are considered *jiuto* (impure) and must in extreme cases leave the house for a few days in order not to sully the purity of their husbands. There is, however, another side to this: women are not permitted to prepare food during menstruation and are allowed to rest while their husbands do the cooking.

There is still a much higher level of illiteracy among women. Increasing access to education has, however, improved the position of women. A good education ensures that a daughter will make a better marriage. Wealthy and high-caste women are not generally expected to work. In some cases a husband might lose face if his wife worked.

Divorce is very uncommon. It is difficult for a divorced woman to return to her original family and she will be expelled by her husband's. Children may remain with their mother until the age of six, after which they "belong" to their father.

Widows are traditionally shunned by society, especially in more remote districts. They may well be thrown out by their husband's family as an extra mouth to feed. It is believed they are responsible for their husbands' deaths, and in extreme cases they may even be called witches.

In marked contrast, in the business world of Kathmandu and in increasing numbers of governmental and national agencies and organizations, women are emerging as CEOs and holding other senior posts. In 2015, Bidhya Devi Bhandari was elected president of the Federal Democratic Republic, and is Nepal's first female head of state.

Attitudes to women are beginning to change now that more women contribute to the family income, particularly in the fast-changing social dynamics of Kathmandu, and in conjunction with the implementation of aspects of the 2015 Constitution. Western women are unlikely to experience discrimination, apart from occasionally being ignored if in the company of a man.

SAME-SEX LOVE

At a constitutional level, Nepal is by far the most advanced country of South Asia in the struggle for human rights and equality, and for Lesbian Gay Bisexual and Trans (LGBT) human rights. There is even an annual LGBT Pride festival that takes place in Kathmandu at the time of the Gai Jatra festival (see page 91). That said, there is widespread cultural and social rejection of same-sex love and gender minorities, and LGBT people face discrimination, rejection by family and friends, and often extreme forms of persecution, such as being hounded out of jobs or subjected to physical violence. Nepal has one of the highest suicide rates in the world, with LGBTs in particular at risk.

The Blue Diamond Society (BDS) and the Federation of Sexual and Gender Minorities Nepal (FSGMN) are active in supporting LGBT community members and accomplishing policy change on Nepal LGBT human rights. Same-sex marriage remains illegal though, and the implementation of LGBT human rights legislation is only slowly taking place.

It's worth noting that the impact of the caste system is much more muted in the LGBT community. Prejudice, hostility, and the need for safety bind people together and largely dissolve caste differences, as LGBT Bahun, Chhetri, or Dalit all share the same experience.

ATTITUDES TOWARD CHILDREN

Despite their love of children, many Nepalis do not
see anything wrong in children being put to work,
although such industries as carpet makers are now
careful not to show children working. You will not
infrequently see children working as vendors, in the
kitchens of hotels, or sitting under a tailor's sewing
machine on the street, helping out with hand stitching.
Many may also be employed as servants. What
Westerners may see as child labor and exploitation
is likely to be seen in Nepal as giving a poor child
a chance, as they in many cases live in and are fed,
clothed, and possibly even sent to school by their
employers.

ATTITUDES TOWARD NEIGHBORING COUNTRIES

Strong ethnic, religious, and trade links have existed
for centuries between Nepal and Tibet. Tibetans are
perceived to be industrious and skilled tradesmen.
Thanks to the efforts of refugees from the Chinese
annexation of Tibet in 1951 carpets are now one of
Nepal's most successful exports.

Nepalese attitudes toward their Indian neighbors
are ambivalent. Historically, Nepalis are wary of their
much more powerful southern neighbor. Several of the
key demands of the Maoist insurgents relate to Nepal's
"antinational and dangerous" relationship with India.

Indian investors are often perceived as neocolonialist predators exploiting cheap Nepali labor and exerting too much influence on politics and society. It does not help that many Indian nationals have been settling in the Terai, competing for ever scarcer land with Nepalis who have come down from the mountains. If anything goes wrong or missing, there is a tendency to blame unknown Indian scapegoats while sadly there still exists a phenomenon of lame beggars coming in to Nepal from India, such as in the tourist areas of Kathmandu, to seek money.

On the other hand, Indian investment in Nepal is huge; India is one of the country's most important trading partners and markets, and Indians make up the biggest single group of tourists entering the country each year, particularly for Hindu pilgrimage sites such as Pashupatinath (Kathmandu), and Janakpur (Terai). There is also a large Nepali diaspora in India, and intermarriage is not uncommon. Much of the Terai has an Indian "feel," with families, customs, and languages straddling the border.

ATTITUDES TOWARD OTHERS

Nepalis are fiercely proud of their sovereignty and do not take kindly to interference of any sort. Foreigners are not permitted to buy land or property in Nepal and there are restrictions on the length of time foreigners may legally reside in the country. These regulations were introduced to prevent outside influence becoming too strong, but will probably change in the process of the Federal Democratic Republic of Nepal seeking to achieve Developed Nation Status by 2032.

However, the fact that Nepal was never a colony means that people are not suspicious of foreigners as they might be in other developing countries. Westerners are met with a refreshing openness and self-confidence based on equality.

Theoretically, Muslims and Europeans fall into a lower-caste category, but not to such a level that physical contact with them necessarily leads to impurity. Some members of higher castes may not accept water from a Westerner, and in certain remote districts Westerners may be treated as untouchables and not permitted to enter the houses of higher-caste people. Visitors should in any case be careful not to offend religious sensibilities. Entry to certain temples is forbidden for non-believers. You should always wait to be invited into people's kitchens, as the hearth is sacred. Your presence may be considered to sully the purity of the kitchen, necessitating a religious ceremony performed by a high priest to restore it.

Normally, however, you will be met with friendliness and smiles wherever you go. Nepalis are courteous and extremely hospitable. They are not, as in some other countries, generally out for what they can get. They will treat you with respect, and with interest rather than envy. And they will expect respect in return.

Despite the ethnic mix and history of cultural tolerance, the attitudes of some traditionally minded Nepalis are not without a racial element. Among such sections of Nepali society, darker skins are associated with "inferiority," while fairer complexions are considered desirable in potential marriage partners.

Nepal gained a slightly permissive reputation during the 1970s, when Kathmandu's Jhhonchen Tole became a stop on the international hippie trail and acquired the name "Freak Street." In marked contrast, the hashish-smoking *sadhus* of Pashupatinath do so for religious reasons. They are respected for their asceticism, humility, and wisdom.

People dress modestly, conservatively, and, especially women, generally in Nepali style, that is, a sari or *kurta suruval/daura suruwal* (long tunic over trousers), particularly in the countryside, with further variants of traditional costume in the High Himalayas. Western attire is more common in the towns and urban areas, particularly Kathmandu.

Displays of physical intimacy in public are taboo for anyone. While same-sex love and partnerships used to be illegal, thanks to the work of the LGBT Blue Diamond Society and its founder Sunil Babu Pant, both the 2007 Interim Constitution and later the 2015 Constitution include a specific LGBT legal and human rights provision that also extends to gender minorities.

It is considered perfectly normal for friends of the same sex to hold hands in public (but definitely not same-sex partners) as the engrained cultural tradition of brotherhood and of sisterhood is a dynamic and important social norm. This is also seen in mass group same-sex dancing across most of Nepal's different ethnicities, for example famously in the Teej (page 91).

NEPALI PERSPECTIVES ON TIME

Time is *not* of the essence in Nepal. If you drop in on someone, they will expect to make you tea and spend time with you. Conversely, if you receive an unexpected visitor, they may not understand if you are too busy to spend time with them. This has to do with Nepali ideals of hospitality, a concept that is revered and has spiritual significance in real day to day life, and the belief that the opportunity to do what is meant to be done will come around again.

It can be difficult to persuade people to commit themselves to a specific time. Partly because of the *aphno manche* system, there is little competition between craftsmen, and so little incentive for them to improve their services or get jobs done rapidly; but this is because creative work is approached not "as a job that one is paid for" but as an act linked to spiritual inspiration and guidance from the gods and goddesses. For visitors from the West and other countries where twenty-first century consumerist and materialist perspectives and priorities predominate, this aspect of traditional Nepali culture can be educational and inspiring. The Nepalese word for "tomorrow" is *bholi*; "the day after tomorrow" is *parsi*. What you are most likely to hear when you ask when something will be done is *bholi-parsi*, however. Although literally meaning in Nepali "tomorrow or the day after," it commonly signifies the very non-committal "in due course."

CHAPTER THREE

RELIGION, CUSTOMS, & TRADITIONS

Until officially secularized in April 2006, Nepal was the only Hindu kingdom in the world, its king held to be a reincarnation of Vishnu. Hinduism in Nepal, since the lifetime of the Lord Buddha, has always has always been interwoven with Buddhism. Moreover the forms of Buddhism that took shape to the north, in Tibet, continue to thrive in the Sino-Tibetan ethnicities of the Himalayan regions of Nepal. Both creeds have incorporated aspects of each other as well as ancient indigenous beliefs connected to deities specific to Nepal, making religion in the country a unique and complex blend of traditions, beliefs, practices, and rituals, in which Shamanism and Tantrism are important strands.

Religious tolerance and mutual respect allow Hindus, Buddhists, Muslims, and others to live together in peace, although conversions are not officially recognized, and proselytization, as we have seen, is illegal. According to the September 2015 Constitution: "Acts leading to conversions from one religion to another [are] banned, and acts that undermine or jeopardize the religion of another prohibited. At the same time the constitution declares the nation to be secular and neutral toward all religions." This approach, while clearly frustrating to evangelists and proselytizers, has been a major factor in enabling Nepal to avoid the forms of division and strife between religions found in other lands.

According to the census of 2001, 80.6 percent of Nepalis gave their religion as Hindu, 10.7 percent as Buddhist, 4.2 percent as Muslim, and 4.5 percent to other religions. This chapter concentrates mainly on Hinduism and Buddhism, the two religions that do most to define the nature of the country and its people, but with reference to ancient indigenous beliefs too.

HINDUISM IN NEPAL

Unlike other world religions, Hinduism cannot be traced back to a particular founder. In the absence of a strict dogma, it has assimilated various currents of thought over millennia, to a certain extent incorporating other creeds rather than suppressing them, without seeming to discard very much on the way. The result is a highly complex philosophical, religious, and social system. For Hindus the religion has a clear underlying structure, focusing as much on actions as on beliefs. Thus, people with apparently contradictory beliefs may still consider themselves to be Hindus. Historically, Hinduism developed in three stages.

The Vedic Era

This period dates from around 1500 to 900 BCE, when Aryan invaders swept into the Indian sub-continent from Central Asia to subjugate the native Dravidians. Their Vedic nature gods, such as Surya (sun) and Indra (rain), were immortalized in the four *Vedas* (Books of Wisdom), the earliest Hindu scriptures, thought to have been written between the twelfth and eighth centuries BCE. Four broad caste groups were established at this time: Brahmins (priests, called Bahuns in Nepal), Chhetris (warriors and rulers), Vaisyas (traders and farmers), and Sudras (artisans and menial workers).

The Brahmanist Period

This age (900–500 BCE) was characterized by the increasing importance of ritual and priests. By ensuring that only the highest caste, the Brahmins, were responsible for the carrying out of religious ceremonies, the Aryans were able to maintain their hold on power. It is no coincidence that Buddhism developed toward the end of this age, finding ways to salvation without dependence on priests, and whose core spiritual philosophy rejected the concept of caste.

Modern Hinduism

The form of Hinduism generally practiced today developed around 400–200 BCE as a reaction to this ascetic movement and in a return to the original values of the *Vedas*. Hinduism is practiced in many lands across south and southeast Asia, without counting the diaspora of Hindu communities in other lands, including

Western countries. However, only Nepal and India have substantial Hindu majorities. These two countries share a territory, the Ganges and its tributaries (most of which rise in the Nepali Himalayas), which constituted much of the cradle of ancient Vedic civilization.

Although Nepal's territory is very small in comparison to India, like the latter it has a multitude of different forms of Hinduism, from exoteric to esoteric, as does the religion with the next largest following, Buddhism, substantially interconnected from its inception with Hinduism. In Nepal during the period 2008–18 the percentage of followers of Hinduism of any description fell from 89 percent to 80 percent, while the numbers of Buddhists almost doubled to 10 percent. To put this in perspective, centuries earlier the vast majority of people in the Indian subcontinent were followers of Buddhism, which, particularly during the reign of the emperor Ashoka (273–232 BCE), was in the ascendant.

Fundamental Beliefs of Hindus

Hindus believe in the existence of an impersonal, all-pervading reality, Brahman. He provides a continuous, endless cycle of genesis and demise. Brahman is manifested on Earth as the eternal order of *dharma*, which makes life and the universe possible. The entire living world is understood as a single organism with different but related life forms, all subordinate to the principles of creation and destruction. Humankind is high up in the rankings, but not the crown of creation. Our world is the center of the cosmos. There is also an underworld full of devils and hells, while the gods are to

---

SOME CORE FEATURES OF HINDUISM IN NEPAL

- Reverence for the *Vedas*
- Belief in the concept of God (Brahman), and by extension gods and goddesses
- Emphasis on the importance of rituals
- Acceptance of the philosophical concepts of the final *Veda*, the *Upanishad*
- Belief in reincarnation
- Belief in the four *ashrams* (age-based stages of life: student, householder, retired, renunciate)—part of the *dharma* system
- Belief in the concept and role of *guru*/ spiritual teacher
- Hospitality: "*Athithi Devo Bhava*" (Guest is God)

---

be found in various heavens above the Earth. They, too, are subject to the cyclical principle.

The soul is also part of the cycle and therefore eternal. As it can move between different forms of life, there is a close relationship between humans and animals, reflected in such gods as Hanuman the monkey god, and Ganesh the elephant-headed god.

The soul of each individual being is like a lost fragment of the soul of the universe. The ultimate goal is to attain *moksha*, or release from the eternal cycle, when the individual soul is reunited with the absolute soul (Brahman). In order to achieve this, it must go through a series of rebirths, known as *sansara*, ideally moving up the social scale with each reincarnation. Where the soul next finds a home depends on how well the living being fulfils its *dharma* in its current existence.

This causal correlation, or *karma*, is one of the most important fundamentals of Hinduism and it is deeply anchored in the caste structure. Each person has a fixed position in the social hierarchy, determined by the extent to which the soul conformed to *dharma* in its previous existence. Thus a low-caste Hindu must accept his or her lot to atone for sins in a previous life. By following *dharma* dutifully a person may hope to achieve a higher status in the next life.

Hindu Religious Obligations

Hindus have certain obligations or debts. One is to the gods, and should be met through daily acts of worship, the following of rituals, and the offering of sacrifices. Second, their debt to "the sages" is to be met by studying the *Vedas* and adhering to the rules of the caste system; and the third is an obligation to their ancestors to marry within their caste to produce a male heir who will carry on the family line and, most importantly, perform the cremation rites necessary for ascension into the next life. These obligations are not universal, but particular to each individual in his or her personal situation. A Bahun priest must not therefore eat meat or take life, as this would destroy the purity he needs in order to be able to worship on behalf of his community. The Chhetri or warrior caste, on the other hand, must protect others; thus, it is not inconceivable that they may take life.

THE HOLY COW

The veneration of the cow is an important tenet of Hinduism. The cow is regarded as a sacred symbol of motherhood and fertility, and the killing of a cow, even by accident, is considered to be one of the most serious of religious transgressions. It is common in rural districts, but sometimes in roads in major towns and cities too, to see cows on roadways resting, with traffic carefully bypassing them. This iconic Nepali and South Asian sight reminds us that reverence for the spiritual is part of daily life, and does not just take place in temples.

The Hindu Gods of Nepal

Hinduism is both monotheistic and polytheistic. It incorporates a vast pantheon of gods and goddesses with different attributes, and yet these are merely the expression of different aspects of a single, supreme absolute, Brahman. The Hindu *Trimurti* ("trinity" of gods) symbolizes the three aspects of the omnipresent Brahman: Brahma is the creator of the universe; Vishnu its preserver; and Shiva its destroyer.

While most Hindus recognize the existence and significance of many gods, no one is under any obligation to worship any particular god. The most popular are Vishnu, Shiva, and the Mother Goddess, Devi. All have both positive and negative characteristics, and multiple forms. Their essentially human strengths and failings make them easy to identify with, and individuals generally have a favorite. Temples tend to be devoted to a single deity.

Brahma is rarely worshiped directly (creation being largely finished with). Vishnu sometimes appears as Narayan, the "sleeping Vishnu," recumbent on the cosmic ocean. He is also worshiped in the form of ten incarnations, including Krishna, the popular cowherd hero of the great Hindu epic the *Mahabharata*, Rama, hero of the *Ramayana*, and the Buddha: this last represents an attempt on the part of Hinduism to incorporate aspects of Buddhism.

Shiva is both creator and destroyer. He is often symbolized by a phallic lingam for his creative role, and has many different manifestations. In a good mood he appears as the peaceful Pashupati, lord of the beasts and one of the most popular gods in Nepal. Pashupatinath in Kathmandu is the most important Hindu temple in Nepal, drawing pilgrims from all over Nepal and India. Shiva is also known as Nataraja, the cosmic dancer who created the world and was believed to smoke hashish. Shiva in a filthy mood is Bhairab, often featured with multiple arms and weapons, standing over a corpse, and wearing a necklace or belt made of skulls.

The iconography associated with each god helps with identification. Each god has a "vehicle" (animal) and a *shakti* (consort or female counterpart) with certain attributes and abilities. Each is often also depicted holding a typical object or symbol—for example, a conch shell or lotus flower for Vishnu, a trident for Shiva.

Part of the Pashupatinath Temple complex on the banks of the Bagmati River.

Shaktis are the creative or reproductive energies of the gods, without which they are neither complete nor effective. *Shaktis* also have different manifestations. If Shiva is the god of both creation and destruction, it is often his *shakti*, Parvati, manifesting as the goddesses Durga or Kali, who actually does the destroying. Kali demands blood sacrifices and wears a garland of skulls. The second-most important Hindu temple in Nepal, at Dakshinkali just outside Kathmandu, is dedicated to Kali. Animal sacrifices take place here regularly throughout the year.

Shaktism (also better known as Tantrism) is a mystical form of both Buddhism and Hinduism particularly important in Nepal, in which believers seek salvation through certain rituals and esoteric practices, including sexual rites. A number of uniquely Nepali deities, most famously the Kumari, or Living Goddess, relate to Nepali Shaktism.

How Nepali Hindus Worship

Religion is an integral part of daily life for most Nepalis. The day often starts with an act of worship. If you stay near a temple, you can expect to be woken early by the bells, the ringing of which brings the worshiper closer to the gods. Many Nepalis have a small shrine at home, where *puja* (offerings) of rice or fruit and colored powder are made each day to the favorite deity of the household. It is generally the wife who makes these offerings. The powder is then used to administer a *tikka* (red mark) to the forehead of each member of the family as a sign of daily communion with the gods. This takes

place after washing and before eating. Guests are also likely to receive a *tikka*.

The temple is not only a place of worship but also a cultural center and meeting place. Although the inner courtyards of certain temples (Pashupatinath in Kathmandu, for example) are off-limits to non-Hindus, visitors are generally welcome and may even be invited to participate. Shoes should be removed before entering. Especially at temples dedicated to female deities, goats or chickens are sacrificed on special occasions.

The veneration of priests includes the offering of hospitality to priests and *sadhus* or *gurus* (teachers and spiritual guides). These are individual, male ascetics who have embarked upon a spiritual search and live from alms. They go from door to door, dressed in little more than a loincloth, and with few possessions

apart from a small cooking pot in which they collect handfuls of rice. They are respected figures, not beggars, and perform spiritual ceremonies if required.

Some of the most fundamental ceremonies for every Hindu are those associated with rites of passage. These start at birth with a blessing and naming ceremony, and continue the first time a baby is fed solid food (rice). Relatives and friends bring money and gifts and the baby receives a spoonful of rice from each guest. Later there are ceremonies to mark the first time a boy has his hair cut, and purification after a girl first menstruates. Other significant ceremonies are marriage, blessings upon a pregnancy, and finally, cremation, including the sprinkling of ashes on a holy river, and annual offerings to deceased ancestors. If possible, these last should be made by the eldest son, so that the soul of his father can pass from a state of limbo to rebirth.

Newar girls also celebrate *Ihi*, their symbolic marriage to the god Vishnu, between the ages of seven and eleven, which is to protect them from the stigma of widowhood. Married to an immortal god they cannot become widows.

BUDDHISM IN NEPAL

The birthplace of the Lord Buddha, Lumbini, is in Nepal, and as a consequence Nepal is regarded as a sacred land. Lumbini is one of the four most important pilgrimage sites of Buddhism; the other three are located in modern India. There are many forms of Buddhism in Nepal, from the earliest school to the exclusively meditation-orientated form (Vipassana meditation), which non-Nepali students can experience.

Buddhism in fact follows the same goal as Hinduism, from which it originated, and adheres to the principles of *karma* and reincarnation. It dispenses with the mediating role of priests and the caste system, however.

The religion's founder, Siddhārtha Gautama Buddha (c. 563–483 BCE), gave up worldly goods and pleasures and become an ascetic in the search for enlightenment. When this failed to work, he developed his "Middle Way" of meditation. He recognized "Four Noble Truths," teaching that life means suffering because of our sensual desires and the illusion that they are important. We can only escape this suffering by renouncing the pleasures of the world and by following the "Eightfold Path" of right understanding, right aspiration, right speech, right action, right livelihood, right effort, right thought, and right contemplation to selflessness and liberation from suffering. Salvation of the soul is achieved when the soul enters *nirvana* (literally "drifting/fading away"), a state in which all earthly desires are extinguished and the cycle of reincarnation is broken. To achieve *nirvana* it is necessary to go through a series of rebirths, but this is not simply fate, because what people do

in one life will influence what role they play in the next.
In contrast to Hinduism, the individual soul is not eternal
and unchangeable, but formed according to the laws of
karma when a person dies.

The Buddha himself never wrote down his teachings,
and two main forms of Buddhism developed after his
death. The first, the Hinayana, or "Lesser Vehicle," held
that it was the role of the individual to attain *nirvana*.
Later, in the first century BCE, the Mahayana, or "Greater
Vehicle," school of Buddhism emerged, pleading for the
collective attainment of *nirvana*. The most important
change they made was in introducing the Bodhisattva:
someone who has achieved enlightenment but who elects
not to enter *nirvana* in order to show others the way to
salvation. The most revered of these is Avalokiteshvara,
representing compassion. Over time, Mahayana
Buddhism incorporated not only the Bodhisattvas,
but also various Hindu gods. Their representations in
temples and shrines in combination with rituals and a
rich mythology made them more accessible to people
than the abstract philosophy of "the enlightened one."

Vajrayana (thunderbolt, or Diamond Vehicle) or
Tantric Buddhism began to be practiced in Nepal from
around the eighth century CE. This is an esoteric school
in which mystical forces, rituals, and sexual practices
play an important role. Tantric rituals have also had great
influence on some forms of Hinduism, and in Nepal
Tantric Hinduism exists alongside Tantric Buddhism.
Tantrism is based on the interwovenness of all things.
Devotees are led to enlightenment through reading
scriptures, reciting holy *mantras* (sacred words used as

The embrace of the Buddhist deity Samvara and his consort Vajrahjavi is a metaphor for the union of wisdom and compassion.

an object of concentration), contemplating *mandalas* (holy pictures of gods or their symbols), and performing ritual movements (*mudra*). Other more esoteric practices affirm the spiritual role of human sexuality, as seen in many ancient sculptures of temples and shrines.

Prevalent in parts of northern Nepal and the Kathmandu valley is Tibetan Buddhism, under the spiritual leadership of the Dalai Lama. It draws on aspects of the ancient "Bon" religion of Tibet, the religious practices of the Himalayan peoples (shamanism, animism, nature religions, and others), and the "vehicles" of Mahayana and Vajrayana Buddhism.

How Buddhists Worship

In a spiritual practice called circumambulation, it is usual to walk clockwise around all Buddhist temples, because this follows the sun's course: Buddha is the sun of enlightenment in people's hearts. Prayer wheels are a feature of all Buddhist temples. These often elaborately carved metal cylinders contain rolls of paper wrapped round an axis, on which holy *mantras* are written many times. The wheels are often mounted in rows near the entrance to *stupas*, to be turned by people during circumambulation as a means of spreading spiritual blessings and well-being. The prayer wheels, flags, *thangkas* (religious paintings), and murals in monasteries are all seen as aids to meditation, bringing the devout closer to the divine. Everywhere you will hear the *mantra* "*Om mani padme hum*," "Praise to the jewel in the lotus."

SYNCRETISM

If religious tolerance is a feature in Nepal, so too is syncretism; indeed the former may be said to be one of the major outcomes of the latter. Hinduism and Buddhism have intermingled in Nepal to such a degree over the centuries that if you ask a Nepali if he is Hindu or Buddhist, you may well get the answer "Yes!"

Hindus and Buddhists in Nepal share temples, gods, symbols, and festivals. Hindu gods may be depicted in Buddhist temples, and Buddhist *stupas* may be found in Hindu temples. In Pashupatinath, the Shiva lingam is covered once a year with a mask of the Buddha. At the Buddhist *stupa* of Swayambhunath, Hindus worship the god of Swayambhunath as "Sambu" (Shiva). For Buddhists, Swayambhu is the Buddha. Buddhists see an aspect of the Bodhisattva Avalokiteshvara in Lokeshvara, "the lord of the world," whereas Hindus see him as a manifestation of Shiva in the form of a Buddhist god.

The goddesses Kali and Durga also often merge with the Buddhist goddess Tara, the most important female Bodhisattva. Female goddesses are often perceived to be variants of the Divine Mother, particularly in Tantrism. The erotic carvings on the roof beams of many temples are also common to both religions and stem from Hindu tantrism, which was adapted by Buddhism.

Nowhere is the syncretism between the two religions clearer than among the Newar people of the Kathmandu valley. Newars may be Hindus or Buddhists. In practice the issue of "which religion" does not seem relevant to many Newars. They worship a plethora of hybrid gods that may or may not be recognized by purists of one religion or the other! Marriage between Hindus and Buddhists of the same caste is not a problem. Newar Hindus may feel closer to Newar Buddhists than to other Nepali Hindus, simply because they speak the same language and share their cultural heritage.

ANCIENT INDIGENOUS BELIEFS UNIQUE TO NEPAL

Aspects of shamanic or animist religions continue to be practiced, especially in remote rural areas. Tantrism, also known as Shaktism, the most characteristic form of Hinduism and Buddhism in Nepal, contains elements of these. The cycles of creation and destruction are interlinked, part of the order of Nature and the Cosmos, and bound up with the realization of spiritual enlightenment. These esoteric forms of religion and spirituality are akin to some facets of Tibetan Buddhism.

There are also a number of deities unique to Nepal, particularly in the Kathmandu valley (Kumari being the most famous). These commonly have shamanic characteristics and purposes.

Matsyendranath: considered by Newaris as the Protector of Kathmandu valley.

Bhimsen: God of Income, and a local deity of the Kathmandu valley. Dharahara, the famous iconic tower of Kathmandu destroyed in the 2015 earthquake, was also known as Bhimsen's Tower.

Kumari: The Living Goddess.

THE CULT OF THE LIVING GODDESS

The cult of the Living Goddess, or Kumari, among the Newar is one of the most fascinating manifestations of religion in Nepal. The most important Kumari is the Kumari Devi, or "Royal Kumari," who lives in a house known as the Kumari Ghar on the edge of Kathmandu's Durbar Square.

The Kumari is believed to be the incarnation of the goddess Taleju, a manifestation of Durga. Although Taleju is a Hindu goddess, the Kumari is always selected from the Newar Buddhist Sakhya caste of goldsmiths and silversmiths. For Buddhists she is the tantric goddess Vajradevi.

The Kumari is chosen in early childhood from a group of candidates who take part in a secret ritual conducted by priests, which includes being left in a room full of severed water buffalo heads, the theory being that if she is really a reincarnation of the bloodthirsty goddess Durga, she will not mind!

She lives in seclusion in the service of religion, leaving her house very rarely to perform religious duties such as legitimizing the rule of the king by administering a *tikka* to his forehead as a symbol of the Third Eye of Wisdom, at the Indra Jatra festival. She is believed to have great power and is widely worshiped by both Hindus and Buddhists, who will wait under her windows hoping for a glimpse of her. As soon as she begins menstruating or loses blood by injury, she returns to her family and is replaced.

Taleju: a goddess also unique to Nepal. Different, gentler, yet comparable to Durga, Taleju is considered the chief patron of the country. Taleju temples of magnificent design were constructed in the three cities of the Kathmandu valley.

Vishwakarma: presiding deity of all craftsmen of Nepal and India

Swasthani: four-handed goddess unique to Nepal, and celebrated for the granting of wishes.

Yoginis: these four hybrid deities are only found in Nepal, are considered to be practitioners of Yoga.

NON-NEPALI RELIGIONS: ISLAM AND CHRISTIANITY

The first Muslims to arrive in Nepal were traders from Kashmir and India who came between the fifteenth and seventeenth centuries. The descendants of these early Muslim settlers speak Nepali and are not easy to distinguish from high-caste Hindus. After the Indian Mutiny of 1857, many more came north to escape the violence and settled in the Terai. They maintain close links to communities across the border in Bihar and Uttar Pradesh. Unlike in India, in Nepal they and their Hindu neighbors continue to coexist in peace.

There are a small number of practicing Christians in Nepal, who tend to meet in private houses. In recent years, particularly after the earthquake of 2015, there have been issues arising from evangelical activity. In the aftermath, Christian evangelicals came to Nepal to seek to convert Nepalis of Hindu, Buddhist, and other persuasions to Christianity, using controversial inducements such as material incentives. Some earthquake victims were offered assistance with rebuilding their homes *if* they converted to Christianity and became apostates to their religions of birth. The 2015 Constitution of Nepal, we have seen, has a section dealing with the matter.

RELIGIOUS TRADITIONS AND RITES OF PASSAGE

Religion is such an important aspect of life in Nepal that it is sometimes said that "every other building is a temple, and every other day is a festival." There are hundreds of religious festivals throughout the year. Most are related to Hindu or Buddhist gods or tradition, but some honor personal relatives or ancestors, while others mark the passing of the seasons or agricultural cycles. They may be celebrated at temples or other religious sites (such as rivers), or at home. Some are celebrated countrywide, others are regional. Many involve ritual bathing, and most culminate in feasting within the family. They are part of the common heritage, and bring people together whatever their creed or ethnic or cultural background.

Be sure to join in! Nepalese hospitality, inclusiveness, and a genuine eagerness to share their culture mean that you are likely to be invited to participate in proceedings. This can be enlightening, and it is always enjoyable.

Businesspeople or those operating to a tight schedule should be aware that the country can come to a complete standstill for days at a time during festivals. This can be a problem especially during Dashain and Tihar, celebrated in September and late October/early November, when it is traditional for people to return to their ancestral homes or visit family. Some of the most important festivals are given below.

THE NEPALI CALENDAR

Officially Nepal follows the Vikram Sambat solar calendar, which is fifty-seven years ahead of the Gregorian calendar. The Nepalese year begins in mid-April and consists of twelve months that are out of step with the Western ones. Thus the Nepali year 2064 began in April 2007. Most religious festivals, however, are calculated by astrologers according to a lunar calendar, so dates can vary. Things are further complicated by the fact that Newars follow their own calendar, celebrating their New Year in November, and the Tibetan peoples of the mountains follow a different calendar again.

January/February
Basant Panchami marks the beginning of spring and is devoted to Saraswati, the goddess of learning. Schoolchildren make offerings at her shrines.

Losar, the Tibetan New Year, is observed by Tibeto-Burmese people with folk songs and dancing at the new moon in February. Hundreds of lamas and traditionally-dressed Tibetans circumambulate the *stupa* at Bodhnath in Kathmandu.

February/March

Shivaratri brings thousands of *sadhus* and other pilgrims from all over Nepal and India to Pashupatinath. People bathe in the Bagmati. At night, hundreds of oil lamps are lit and an all-night vigil is held.

Also known as the Festival of Colors, **Holi** heralds the beginning of spring and looks forward to the coming harvest. People roam the streets throwing colored powder and water at each other. Foreigners are likely to be special targets. It is all very good-natured, but be prepared to throw your clothes away afterward, or don't go out.

At the festival of **Rato Machhendranath**, the painted wooden image of the god of rain and fruitful grain, who is believed to have influence over the monsoon, is transported around Patan on a tall, precarious-looking chariot that dwarfs the men heaving it along its solid wooden wheels. For Nepali Hindus, Machhendranath is an incarnation of Shiva; for Buddhists he is Lokeshvara, the bodhisattva of compassion, lord of the world. The festival is thus celebrated by both Hindus and Buddhists, and was traditionally attended by the king and the Kumari Devi, who gave the king her blessing.

Giant chariot being prepared for Bisket Jatra in Durbar Square, Bhaktapur.

April/May

Bisket Jatra is the Nepali New Year, which starts at the beginning of the Nepali month Baisakh, more or less in the middle of April. This is an official public holiday. In Bhaktapur the fierce, angry god Bhairab is taken for a ride around the town on another cumbersome chariot. A huge lingam is erected on the riverbank, only to be pulled down again the next day in a tug-of-war.

Mani Rimdu is a three-day Sherpa festival at the full moon in May and celebrates the vanquishing of the ancient Tibetan Bon religion by Buddhism.

Buddha Jayanti is celebrated by both Hindus and Buddhists to mark the birth, enlightenment, and death of Buddha (a reincarnation of Vishnu for Hindus).

July/August

At the festival of **Janai Purnima**, Bahun and Chhetri men change the *janai* (sacred thread) that they wear from left shoulder to right hip to symbolize purity.

Everyone is given a thread to be tied around their wrist on this day as a protective talisman for the rest of the year.

Gai Jatra venerates the cow. The Newar people believe that cows will lead them to the next world after death. Those who have lost relatives during the previous year join a procession of people leading cows through the streets of Kathmandu in order to facilitate their deceased relatives' passage into the next world. Later, people wear cow masks, and the tradition is to exchange silly jokes!

August/September

Teej, dedicated to the Goddess Parvati, is a special, three-day festival for women only, involving a major feast, the *Dar* (so-called after "heavy food" or *daro khana*), followed by rigorous fasting, ritual bathing to wash away sin, and dancing. They pray for the longevity of their husbands and the success of their marriages. After bathing, they traditionally don all the red and gold finery of their wedding day. Western women are welcome spectators and may well be invited to join in. Teej also celebrates the end of the monsoon.

Indra Jatra marks the end of the monsoon and is celebrated enthusiastically by both Hindus and Buddhists. A procession of three golden chariots is taken around the city, carrying the Kumari and her attendants—two boys dressed up as Ganesh and Bhairab. Traditionally the king paid homage to her and was blessed for a further year.

September—December

Dashain, also known as **Bijaya Dashami,** lasts fifteen days and is the most important festival in Nepal. The country virtually shuts down and traffic conditions are chaotic beforehand as everyone makes the effort to get home. People celebrate by eating good food and buying new clothes. It takes place after the monsoon, in late September or early October. It is also known as **Durga Puja**, as it celebrates the slaying of the buffalo demon Mahisasura by this goddess.

Certain days of Dashain are more significant than others. On the first day the devout bathe and plant barley in sand and water taken from the river. On the seventh day, *Fulpati* ("sacred flowers"), flowers are brought from the old palace of Prithvi Narayan Shah at Gorkha to the king at Hanuman Dhoka in Kathmandu. The eighth day is Kala Ratri ("black night"), when eight buffaloes and a hundred-and-eight goats are decapitated in Durbar Square, Kathmandu, ideally with one chop of the knife.

This is one festival in which it is impossible to avoid guts and gore! Temples are awash in sacrificial blood on the ninth day, when literally thousands of goats meet their end—35 to 40,000 goats are slaughtered on that day in the town of Pokhara alone. The tools of a person's trade (guns for a soldier, a saw for a carpenter) are then sprinkled with sacrificial blood in the hope that Durga will bless their usefulness and accuracy. Blood is also sprinkled on all vehicles, including the aircraft of Nepal Airlines, to safeguard against accidents, and if you take a closer look at the clear, plastic-covered "padlock chains" draped around parked motorcycles and bicycles, you'll find they are actually the cleaned out intestines of a goat!

Not many Nepalis eat a lot of meat but at Dashain most people will have goat for dinner. Family visits are made on the tenth day and parents put *tikkas* on their children's foreheads and young shoots of barley behind their ears or in their hair.

Tihar (the Nepali name for **Deepawali/Divali**), also known as the Festival of Lights, lasts five days and is celebrated toward the end of October or early November. On the first day, crows (messengers of the god of death) are honored. On the second day, dogs, kicked out of the way throughout the rest of the year, are honored for their role in guiding the deceased across the river of the dead; this day is known as "Kukur Tihar" or "Kukur Puja" (*kukur* is the word for dog in Nepali). Cows are garlanded on the third day, bullocks on the fourth, and the fifth day is called Bhai Tikka (Brothers' Day), when sisters honor their brothers with *tikkas* and blessings, and gifts are exchanged.

On the third, most important day, also known as "Lakshmi Puja," people light up their homes with candles and wick lamps in order to usher in Lakshmi, the goddess of wealth. As with many festivals, Tihar ends with a family feast. In Nepal, the festival marks the end of the national lunar calendar, and is auspicious for new beginnings, prosperity, and health.

Sita Bibaha Panchami recalls the marriage of Rama and Sita and is celebrated mainly in the city of Janakpur in the Terai, birthplace of Sita, where it is believed that Sita and Lord Ram were married. In late November or early December thousands of pilgrims converge on Janakpur, ancient capital of the Mithila Kingdom that spanned the Janakpur area and neighboring districts in Nepal, and much of the modern state of Bihar in India.

MAKING FRIENDS

MEETING NEPALIS

Although socializing in Nepal tends to focus on the
extended family, Nepalis also like to spend time with
friends. (In Nepali friends are *sathiharu*, and a friend,
a *sathi*.) Friendship circles are an important part of
Nepali life and social structure. Friends expect to look
after one another, enjoy life together, share significant
moments such as success at school or an engagement, and
support each other in times of need. Women friends are
important in supporting a bride when she leaves home for
good. Later, family may take precedence over friendships,
particularly for women, who generally move away from
their childhood friends upon marriage. Traditionally,
and still important, background (caste) remains a key
factor in any friendship, and political affiliation may also
play a role Close friendship between people of disparate
backgrounds is unusual—although there are exceptions,
as we have seen, such as among those belonging to
minority groups whose experience of prejudice and

Enjoying the view from Swayambhunath *stupa* overlooking Kathmandu.

disempowerment transcends caste and ethnicity—but social media is impacting on this. Friendships between unrelated men and women are also rare, although things are changing, particularly in urban areas.

Socializing takes place mainly at home, although people may meet at cafés or restaurants in urban areas. Increasingly popular venues, especially for the young, are ice-cream parlors or pizzerias. These are places to be seen, whereas more traditional restaurants often offer discreet facilities, with some tables screened off or in small wooden pavilions. People may also congregate at the temple, water pump, or another central place to talk or watch the world go by. On specific occasions or festivals such as Tihar they may meet at the market to admire decorated shop fronts, as well as to "see and be seen."

The vast majority of Nepali people are open and friendly, although you may find yourself worthy of a few stares in areas off the tourist track. Urban, educated Nepalis will engage you in conversation (in English), and you are likely to be accosted by the friendly shouts of children wherever you go. Although a small minority of these might be looking for sweets, pens, or a few hours' employment as a guide, most simply want to practice their English and are genuinely interested in you and where you come from. They are usually also quite happy to answer your questions. Communication with those who have not been to school is obviously more difficult unless you speak Nepali, but any effort to do so is much appreciated, and if you stay anywhere for a while, you will soon find everyone knows you.

If a Nepali person in your home country gives you the contact details of a family member, you can expect to be received by them as a friend. They will do whatever they can to help you, and will probably introduce you to other family members.

It takes time, however, to establish truly close friendships. This is due partly to the language barrier, but to a certain extent also to cultural differences. Conversations may remain at a superficial level for a long time unless there is a particular shared activity or lifestyle (arts, type of work, food interest, for example) or, of course, social media connection. It is probably easiest to get to know people in a working situation, where you automatically have a common purpose and basis for cooperation. Other ways of making friends may be to take some language lessons, possibly from someone equally eager to learn your language, or to suggest cooking together: people are interested in what Westerners eat, and are both delighted and amused to be asked to explain what to do with the various exotic vegetables, fruits, and spices available at the market. Asking about the Nepali names for food types and ingredients is an ideal way of connecting with people.

GREETINGS AND OTHER COURTESIES

To greet and to say good-bye in Nepal you put the palms of your hands together in front of your chest, as if praying, and say *Namaste*. This literally means "I salute the godly in you." Raising the height of your hands shows

increasing respect. You may also say *Namaskar* to show particular respect for someone. "Ladies first" is not a maxim in Nepal. It is polite to greet the oldest members of a group and men first, while superiors are generally greeted first by their subordinates. "Thank you" is *dhanyabaad*, and is always warmly received.

WHAT SHOULD I TALK ABOUT?

If you speak a little Nepali, small talk will do wonders for your language skills. Initial questions, posed by colleagues, neighbors, taxi drivers and shopkeepers, are likely to focus on where you come from, how long you have been in Nepal, what you are there for, your family, your job, and your diet.

A small collection of photographs of your family and home is a useful icebreaker that will stimulate conversation. Once people get to know you a little better, few topics of conversation are off-limits. An element of comparison or finding out about the other culture is inevitable and mutual. Some questions are potentially embarrassing, such as questions about your income, the price of airfares to Nepal, or other comparative costs. Given the income gap, it may be as well to understate certain costs or put things in a cultural perspective.

Sex, same-sex love, and sexual and gender minorities are not subjects that are casually or openly discussed. Nepalis may, however, surprise you with questions on topics of a personal nature such as contraception or infertility (the latter commonly being a reason for immediate divorce in Nepal) as they look for solutions to their problems in Western ideas. Often there is a specific reason for asking, which may be revealed (but don't be overly inquisitive). You should be extremely cautious about broaching subjects such as poverty, dowries, caste, corruption, the Maoist conflict, and politics in general.

HUMOR

Nepalis are easy-going with a ready sense of humor that tends to be quite slapstick. Foreigners may find it lacking in subtlety. Generally, few Nepalis will appreciate irony or black comedy. They take themselves quite seriously and will criticize themselves, but rightly and understandably do not take kindly to being poked fun at (self-ridicule is fine). Non-Nepali or Western caricatures depicting politicians are seen as disrespectful and tactless. Nepalis will not tolerate even light-hearted disrespect toward older members of the family; this is expected of non-Nepalis and Westerners in relation to officers and leaders of political parties, too.

NEPALI HOSPITALITY

Nepalis are extremely hospitable, and will probably press food and drink on you. Sometimes complete strangers will persist in inviting you to their homes. In this case it is probably as well to smile and give a vague answer: "Yes, sometime I'd love to visit you."

The etiquette of eating and drinking can be something of a minefield. If you really do not want to eat anything, smile and explain that you have just eaten. If invited to dinner at someone's house, you will be guest of honor. In a traditional household you would have been served first and given the best. This is changing, however, but may still be encountered, especially in remote rural districts. This, when it occurs, can make you feel uncomfortable, as the whole family will watch you eat. Don't wait for your host to begin—only once he is sure you are enjoying your meal will the man of the house join in, followed by the family and the children.

The traditional method of eating in Nepal dispenses with cutlery, and only the right hand is used. There is quite an art to eating with the thumb and two fingers of your right hand (the left is used for "other business" and is thus unclean), particularly when sitting cross-legged on the floor with your plate in front of you. Although no one will be offended if you ask for a spoon (knives and forks are less likely to be available), the Nepalis appreciate your making an effort to eat as they do. Eating with your mouth open and smacking noisily with your lips is quite acceptable—indeed, even a sign that you are enjoying your meal and that you feel at ease.

Avoid taking huge amounts on to your plate, as anything that has been on your plate is *jiuto* (unclean) and will be thrown away if you do not eat it. Be careful not to touch anyone else's glass or plate and certainly not their food, as this would also be *jiuto*. Do not under any circumstances step over anyone else or anyone else's plate, as this would show great disrespect.

You may be offered *raksi* to drink. This is a distilled alcoholic beverage of unpredictable strength, often home-brewed, and to be treated with caution. Often it will be passed around a party in a teapotlike metal vessel with a long narrow spout. The idea is to pour the liquid into your mouth without touching the spout: any bottle you touch with your lips is *jiuto* for other people. Jugs of water may also be passed around in this way. There are popular beers such as Gorkha, and also the rice beer, Chang. A beverage that is famous but not easy to find outside traditional venues is *tongba*, a fermented millet drink served in a distinctive bamboo flagon known as a *dhungro* and consumed at room temperature. The *dhungro* holds a metal container of millet that is topped up with hot water (*taato paani*); drunk through a straw, this drink is strong and tends to grow on you.

If you finish everything on your plate, you will be given more. The polite way of showing you have had enough is to leave a little on your plate. Your hosts will appreciate your saying "*Dherai mitho*" ("Very tasty") or "*Ekdam mitho cha*" ("That was delicious").

People welcome return invitations and are interested in what you might offer them. Check beforehand whether they eat meat as many are vegetarian. Avoid beef in a majority Hindu country, and pork too.

WHAT SHOULD I WEAR?

It is always best to err on the side of modesty and formality when choosing what to wear in Nepal. Nepalis dress up to go out. Nakedness is frowned upon, and although Nepalese women may display bare tummies between their blouse and sari, their legs and shoulders are always covered. Women should certainly wear long trousers or skirts. Coolest are often the Nepali-style *Daura Suruwal*—long, fine cotton trousers with a long tunic over the top—and no one will think it strange to see a Westerner in this attire. Indeed, the Nepalis are a very inclusive people, and many are delighted to see their guests in Nepali clothing, especially at festivals. Women will probably be quite honored to be asked for their help in getting you into a sari.

Ties are not necessary except for very formal occasions—indeed, they are impractical in the heat—but a collar is advisable. The traditional *topi* (cloth hat) worn by men is a sign of respectability and should only be worn if you have been given or invited to wear one.

Shoes are considered dirty and should always be removed when entering someone's house.

GIFTS

A gift will not be expected if you are invited to visit a Nepali family, but flowers, fruit, chocolate, or homemade cakes are always appreciated, as is in particular a present of anything from your home country. If you stay with anyone for a while and take photographs while you are there, a small collection of these, particularly those showing both you and your hosts, is likely to go over very well. Books can also make appropriate presents.

A good present for a business contact is a bottle of whiskey, although you should check first whether they drink alcohol. You should avoid gifts made of leather, especially cowhide (as with the prohibition on eating beef, for Hindu religious regions), and anything black or white, as these are considered unlucky colors. White is the color of mourning.

NEIGHBORS

Most expatriates and wealthier Nepalis live in houses surrounded by walled gardens or yards, and you are unlikely to have much to do with your neighbors except to exchange greetings, unless you actively seek their company. However, don't be surprised if a few are bold enough to walk in unexpectedly—doorbells and the concept of knocking before entering are almost unknown.

Noise can be a cause of conflict between neighbors. It is as well to remember that the Nepalis rise at dawn. Half-past four in the morning is not too early for them to start going about their daily business.

Occasionally, private individuals may mark a forthcoming marriage or the anniversary of the death of a loved one by holding a special festival and *puja* (act of devotion or offering). A priest is invited to their house to lead purification ceremonies that include loud prayers, chanting, and music broadcast to the entire neighborhood by means of a loudspeaker. There is little you can do about this. Complaints are unlikely to be understood and you will probably be invited to join in. Such purification festivals can last up to a week.

EXPATRIATE ASSOCIATIONS

Expatriate communities in Nepal are small and largely concentrated in Kathmandu. Individual embassies can provide information about cultural associations. The British Council, Alliance Française, and Goethe Institute all offer library facilities and cultural programs in Kathmandu.

SPORTS AND OTHER VENUES

The facilities you might visit in Western countries in order to meet people, such as sports or other clubs, are still quite rare outside Kathmandu and Pokhara. Even where they exist, most of the people you will meet there are likely to be other expatriates. Nepali women are even less likely than men to engage in sports. Having said that, groups of men and boys playing cricket or football in open spaces may be quite happy to let you join in, while providing a football is one fast way to acquire a young fan club! Volleyball is particularly popular in Nepal, and needs less space than cricket or football to be played.

For LGBT visitors, Megna Lama's Pink Tiffany Bar and Restaurant in Thamel is popular with both the local and international LGBT community and generally with people from Nepal's art, film, and fashion worlds.

CHAPTER FIVE

THE NEPALIS AT HOME

Nepali life centers on home and the family. Traditionally, several generations of a family live in the same house, with children sleeping in their parents' rooms for years with little space and no privacy. There is great interdependence, and a strict hierarchy and respect for age seniority dictate that even adult children may still ask their parents for permission to do things.

Much of life spills out on to the street, which clearly cements the feeling of importance of the community, and generally speaking inhibits social isolation.

NEPALI HOUSING

Generally built in traditional styles with regionally available materials, Nepali houses are as varied as the country's climate and terrain. This said, travelers to Nepal will increasingly see, in Kathmandu and to a lesser extent in the major cities and towns, the

House in the Khumbu Valley at the foot of Mount Everest in northeastern Nepal.

building of ultra-modern high-rise buildings, particularly office blocks with shimmering exteriors.

The standard of housing reflects extreme differences in wealth: some wealthy Nepalis live in luxurious mansions in walled compounds, and growing numbers of middle class people have homes and apartments with all mod cons. In contrast, the poorest—often former bonded laborers—are forced to reconstruct their shelters on the dried-up riverbed each year after the monsoon, using driftwood, plastic bags, and other debris. What you will not see in Nepal are the vast shantytowns found on the edges of some African or South American cities.

Houses reflect the fact that much of Nepali life is conducted out of doors. Most are simple, rectangular constructions featuring two or three small rooms, often one behind the other and connected by a corridor which may be on the outside of the house. Staircases are also often external. An end room facing on to the street sometimes houses a small shop. Many houses look half-built: metal stays are left sticking out of their flat roofs to allow for upward expansion at a later date.

Architectural Delights

For students and lovers of classical South Asian architecture Nepal is a paradise, particularly for the beauty and charm of its Newari houses with their splendid woodwork, with its intricate carvings and patterns. There has been a renaissance in traditional Newar architecture in recent years led by the renowned conservationist architect Rabindra Puri. This movement began with the restoration of a derelict farm in Bhaktapur, itself an almost intact Nepali medieval city, albeit with some damage caused by the 2015 earthquakes. The building (*bhawan*), known as Namuna Ghar ("Model House"), won a UNESCO Asia Pacific Cultural Heritage Award. Like all traditional Newari homes, it is characterized by very low doors and the extensive use of decorative carved woodwork, almost Tolkienesque in impact.

In the homes of those with low incomes kitchens are primitive and may contain only a few pots and pans on open shelves, and a fireplace or kerosene stove. If there is a sink it may well be at ground level, as Nepalis generally wash up or prepare vegetables in a squatting position. Even cold running water in the kitchen is not typical.

Wealthier people might have a (bottled) gas stove and a few electrical goods—an electric rice cooker is a coveted wedding present among the urban wealthy. Dry foods are stored in open sacks to prevent molding in the humid climate. Vegetables and fresh foods are bought or harvested each day as far as possible. People are much more likely to have a television than a fridge, and washing machines are almost unheard of. Instead, washing is done by hand in cold water.

Generally speaking, electricity is only available in urban areas and the Terai. Power outages and surges are frequent. Water shortages also occur. Only wealthier middle-class families have running water in the house.

An indoor lavatory is still a luxury for considerable numbers of Nepalis. Sometimes it is in an outhouse and may well be shared by several families. Western toilets are becoming much more common; traditional toilets (*charpi*) consist of a hole in the ground. Toilet paper is also not common, although it can be bought. Instead, water—there is usually a bucket in the corner of the traditional toilet (if not an outhouse, a very small room in the home)—and the left hand are used. (Which is why it is taboo to offer anyone anything with your left hand.)

In urban areas Western-style bathrooms are on the increase but, generally, the idea of sitting in your own dirty bathwater is disgusting to most Nepalis—running water is important. Many houses have no bathroom at all. Instead, people wash and do their washing at an outside faucet if they have one, otherwise at the local public water pump, even in the middle of the city. By some tacit agreement, men and women use public fountains at different times. Men strip down to a pair of shorts, while women bathe through the fabric of a long petticoat, tied around their chest, leaving their arms free.

The Outdoor Bathroom

Where we lived on the banks of the Rapti River, the men's "bathroom" was upstream from the bridge, the women's downstream. Handfuls of twigs gathered on the way there served as toothbrushes. This was more than a mere bathroom: it was the site of ritual cleansing. Nearby were the cremation *ghats* (platforms). Further downriver still was the local car wash, where it was not unusual to see a truck or bus parked midstream.

Otherwise houses may be spartan by Western standards. Floors are often bare concrete, and furniture is minimal. Beds are simple wooden platforms that may double as sofas. They are more likely to be covered with a straw mat or simple blanket than a mattress. Nepalis typically sit cross-legged on the floor to eat (the rich on sofas), so tables and chairs are relatively unusual.

Most Nepali homes have a house shrine. One room may be set aside to accommodate it, or there may be a small altar set up in the kitchen. The hearth or fire in the kitchen is sacred, so you should never throw rubbish on to the hearth. Always wait to be invited to enter the kitchen or approach the house shrine.

Roof terraces accommodate water tanks and sometimes solar panels, and are used for drying clothes, as well as tomatoes, chilies, and other produce. They also provide an opportunity to take a break from household chores to enjoy the often spectacular panoramic views they command.

Organized refuse collection is being established in Nepal, and ecological awareness is growing as those collecting plastic waste and recyclables generate a modest income and serve the interests of the local community of shopkeepers, residents, and businesses. It is still the practice in remote areas and outside city centers for people to burn their rubbish regularly on the street. Over the past decade there have been major changes in attitude toward litter, with recycling becoming widespread.

HOUSEHOLD DUTIES

Traditionally, women carry out the bulk of household tasks, including the collection of water, firewood, and fodder for animals where required. In wealthy middle-class families, children will not be expected to make much contribution to household duties. In an extended family, the youngest daughter-in-law is the family member lowest in rank. She is likely to be expected to get up first, make everyone else's breakfast, and generally do more than her share of chores.

A decade ago, before the 2015 Constitution and the related political changes and the drive for Developed

Women drawing water from the well in Bhaktapur.

Nation status, an estimated 20 percent of urban families employed a servant (here known as a *didi*) or else children to assist with duties in the house and garden. At that time there were estimated to be more than 56,000 children working as domestic servants in Nepal, with their treatment depending very much on individual circumstances. Only around 30 percent of these children were enrolled in school.

THE NEPALI DAY

In general, Nepalis are up before dawn. The cacophony begins immediately: you are likely to be woken each morning by bells being rung by early worshipers at the local temple, dogs barking, tradesmen calling, the clatter of pots and pans and thundering of buckets

being filled as your immediate neighbors wash up last
night's dishes, and some serious clearing of throats.
(Nepalis consider our habit of blowing our noses into a
handkerchief disgusting, and would expect us to throw it
away. Instead, many Nepalis still spend several minutes
energetically clearing their throats every morning.)

But despite the early commotion, the day begins at a
more leisurely pace than in the West. It may start with a
walk to the local temple. An early breakfast consists of
a cup of *Nepali chiya (masala chiya)*, a sweet spicy tea
made with boiled milk, possibly accompanied by some
puffed rice or *roti*, a flat rice pancake. Thereafter, people
have time to go to the market, get on with household
chores, or do homework. Schools and offices do not
generally open before 10:00 a.m., giving families the
time to enjoy the first of their two main meals of the
day together. In high mountain areas where people are
poorer and rice is scarce, this is likely to be a millet gruel.
Elsewhere, *daal bhat* is the national dish and a twice-
daily ritual.

People wash before and after sitting down to this large
meal of *daal* (lentils) and *bhat* (rice), often accompanied
by spicy vegetables (*tarkari*) and pickles (*achar*). Wealthy
families may have meat or fish as an accompaniment,
particularly on special occasions, when a goat or water
buffalo may be slaughtered. People generally sit cross-
legged on the floor with their plate in front of them, pour
the lentils over their rice, and eat by compressing small
quantities of the rice and lentil mixture into mouthful-
sized balls with the thumb and two fingers of the right
hand. Meat or fish is eaten off the bone.

After *daal bhat*, men will leave for the office, and children for school. Mid-afternoon people eat a snack, *kaajaa*, consisting of puffed rice, a little *dahee* (yogurt) if available, or *roti*, washed down with another cup of *chiya*. Children take a similar snack to school with them.

School generally finishes at 4:00 p.m. After homework and chores, children play among themselves or watch television. Late afternoon, once the heat of the day has begun to subside, is a busy time at the market. Boys and young adults may meet for a game of football or cricket. At around seven the family will convene again for *daal bhat*—their second and last main meal of the day.

Evenings are not long in Nepal, given the time people expect to get up, and outside the tourist areas all is quiet and most lights are out by ten o'clock.

EVERYDAY SHOPPING

Fruit and vegetables are commonly bought from peddlers pushing wheelbarrows or heavily-laden bicycles around the neighborhood, and basics are also available from small corner shops. Most shopping is done at the local *bazaar*, however.

The word "*bazaar*" refers both to the town center and to the "market" as we know it. Few shopping centers or supermarkets exist outside Kathmandu and the other cities and larger towns, so shopping is another aspect of Nepali life that is largely conducted out of doors. Shops are usually small and specialist: you must go to one shop for fruit, another for pulses and flour, another for

Dried fish stall in the busy Asan Tole market in central Kathmandu.

toiletries, and so on. Many craftsmen have names linked
to their skill or business, such as *Tamrakar* (coppersmith
in Nepali). There are often several shops of a particular
type in close proximity, such as goldsmiths, butchers,
or tailors. This is because of the caste and family
background of these professions; the proprietors are
often related.

Away from tourist areas fresh foodstuffs, both
vegetables and meats, are often laid out on the sidewalk.

Some shops sell a wide variety of imported goods
such as pasta, canned foods, breakfast cereals, chocolate,
sweets, and alcohol. These, until recent times, were often
beyond the means of many Nepalis, and may make a
good present. Some commodities considered basics by
most Westerners, including pasta, butter, cheese, and
real coffee, are often not available outside Kathmandu.

The only bread available outside tourist areas is the white, sliced variety with a slightly sweet taste.

As in other areas of life in Nepal, people build up a mutually beneficial relationship with certain shopkeepers whom they consider to be their *aphno manche*. In return for regular patronage and recommendations, they may expect good quality or a good price. It is usual to ask to be shown items, rather than to take them from the shelves yourself, and except where prices are marked, to haggle a little over prices.

CHILDREN

At birth babies are often whisked away from their mother to be examined, washed, and wrapped by their paternal grandmother. She generally plays a key role in bringing up the children within the extended family. Children usually sleep with their parents for several years. Few Nepalis would dream of putting a baby in a crib in a separate room. Small babies are regularly massaged with mustard oil, thought to be good for their skin, and left to bask in the warmth of the sun. Later they may accompany members of the family as they perform daily chores. They do not wear diapers—people just mop up after them where necessary. Older siblings are mobilized at an early age to look out for younger ones. Children are treated as adults from a surprisingly young age, and a sense of respect for all elders, including older siblings, is instilled into them from their earliest years.

While the children of middle-class families are not generally expected to assist with household duties, other children may be required not only to help with housework, but to contribute to the family income from a young age. The vast majority of these are engaged in agriculture, most as unpaid family workers, but large numbers also work in domestic service, factories, as child porters, in shops, hotels, the construction industry, as conductors or ticket collectors on buses, or as street vendors, ragpickers, or beggars. Many find themselves in debt bondage—working to repay debts incurred by their families.

FAMILY EVENTS

At all social levels, the extended family will come together to celebrate family events or religious festivals. People don their best clothes—women their finest saris and jewelry—and *tikkas* are exchanged. Food is always involved and may be presented as offerings to the gods. A goat or water buffalo may be slaughtered. Often the family will also dance or sing.

MARRIAGE

As children grow up, potential marriage partners are discussed. Although love marriages are on the increase, and children may veto a marriage partner, most marriages are still arranged by the parents. Marriage partners are unlikely to be from the same town or known personally to the family beforehand, but are selected on the basis of recommendations from intermediaries, who may be friends or relatives. Same-sex marriage is still illegal in Nepal.

Weddings are elaborate affairs taking place over several days. After a large party hosted by her family, and to which several hundred guests may be invited, a bride is physically picked up by a male blood relative and ceremoniously handed over to her husband and his male relatives to be taken to her new home and family.

Traditions and ceremonies differ according to the social and ethnic background of the couple. In Hindu communities a dowry is usual. In other communities there may be a "bride price." In some communities, brides may be "captured" or elopements may precede a marriage. It is not unheard-of among hill peoples for parents to arrange an elopement to avoid the expense of a wedding!

Bride and groom receiving a flower petal blessing.

EDUCATION

Until the 2015 Constitution era, education was not something to be taken for granted in Nepal. Many children did not attend school regularly. Until recently, of those enrolled fewer than two-thirds completed five years of primary education.

The situation is improving, but access to education is still in many cases heavily dependent on caste, economic status, geographical location, and culture. Education is an aspiration and most middle-class families pay a lot of money to send their children to private schools, where they are expected to study hard. Other children attend local state schools and may be required to contribute to the family income. Not everyone considers it necessary to

Teacher and schoolchildren in Pokhara.

educate daughters, although scholarships providing girls
with free books and uniforms have helped reduce their
disadvantage. Most schools are in urban areas. Children
in remote areas often have to walk miles to get there.

The academic year begins in the Nepali month of
Baisakh (mid-April), and has three terms. There are two
to three weeks' vacation at Dasain and Tihar in October,
two weeks' winter vacation in January, and a four-week
session break in March/April. The school day is generally
from 10:00 a.m. to 4:00 p.m., although some schools in
the Terai operate from 6:00 a.m. to 11:00 a.m. during the
hottest months of the year.

Kindergartens as we know them do not generally
exist. In "nursery" and "kindergarten" classes in private
schools, children from the age of three are taught the

English and Nepali alphabets, numbers 1 to 100, and basic English before being permitted to enter Class 1.

Primary education covers Grades 1–5, from the age of six. Lower Secondary (Grades 6–8) and Upper Secondary (Grades 9–10) follow. In Grade 10 pupils sit for the School Leaving Certificate (SLC). Two years' Higher Secondary education known as "Ten plus Two" may follow. These are semi-specialized (humanities, science, or commerce), and qualify pupils for university. Some professional and technical education is available, but it is relatively new and restricted to the cities.

You will often see signs in Nepal for "English Boarding Schools." These are in fact private day schools in which English is the language of instruction. Many are little more than money-making ventures, but they are successful because the system works for those educated in English. The burgeoning of private schools has improved standards but it has also led to a two-tier system that widens the social and economic divide.

This said, university-age Nepalis demonstrate a focus on and enthusiasm for their studies unusual in other, wealthier countries: education is regarded not as a chore but as a passport not only to personal career advancement but also to broader social development.

UNIVERSITIES

The first language of instruction in Nepal's universities and throughout the higher education system is English, not Nepali. Tribhuvan University, founded in 1959, is the oldest and largest university in Nepal, and in terms of student numbers it is one of the largest in the world. It comprises institutes of medicine, engineering, science and technology, forestry, social sciences, humanities, management, education, and law at locations across the country. Other

Students at Kailali Multiple Campus, Dhangadhi.

universities founded in the 1980s and 1990s are the Mahendra Sanskrit University, Kathmandu University, Pokhara University in the west, Purbanchal University in the east, and the Buddhist foundation, Siddhartha University; recently more universities have been opened, including Lumbini Buddhist University. They offer bachelor's and master's degrees, doctorates, and some lower-level proficiency or technical skills certificates.

Many lecturers have completed master's degrees abroad. University education is generally the preserve of the elite. In some cases graduates may expect a well-paid placement automatically upon graduation. Some graduates who have "made it" do not expect to have to perform menial tasks or physical work again.

Many students belong to the student wings of political parties. Student movements are seen as testing grounds for those aspiring to rise in Nepal's main political parties.

CHAPTER SIX

TIME OUT

LEISURE

Nepalis spend the majority of their leisure time with their family. Weekends are short, given the six-day working week everywhere except the Kathmandu valley, and people do not generally go on vacation. They do make the effort to get to their family home at holiday times. Married women return to their *maiti* (original family) for a break when they can.

You may be invited to join friends on an excursion to a famous religious site or to a local amusement park for a "picnic." It is not sandwiches that are packed up for this (bread not being a constituent of the Nepali diet), but cooking utensils, kerosene stoves, and everything needed to prepare a full-scale freshly cooked *daal bhat*. They may arrange for a car and will aim to arrive early at a designated picnic area, switch on the boom box, and spend the rest of the day cooking, eating, relaxing, possibly dancing, and chatting and catching up on news, as well as enjoying any attractions there might be.

Daal Bhaat, roti, and *tarkari*.

EATING OUT

Daal bhat, the national dish, is wholesome, tasty, and freshly prepared. High-caste Hindus may avoid meat for religious reasons, and not everyone can afford it, so it is usually accompanied by *tarkari* (curried vegetables) and *achar* (spicy pickle). *Roti* are sometimes served instead of rice. *Kwati*, a soup made of different sprouted beans, is often eaten at festivals. *Gundruk*, fermented vegetable leaves (in a container in the ground), is widespread and dried green vegetables are a specialty in the hills.

Newari food is more diverse, especially when it comes to meat, and water buffalo meat in particular. Not much of the animal is wasted, so as well as steak, soup, or meatballs, you may find tongue, liver, or brains on the menu, all cooked in spicy sauces.

Momos with *achar*.

Momos are a sort of Nepali fast food—steamed or fried dumplings filled with buffalo ("Buff") meat, chicken, or vegetables and served with a spicy tomato-based *achar* sauce. *Momos* are perhaps Nepal's favorite type of food, and bear a great resemblance to Chinese dumplings; both can be steamed or fried, but they differ in some of the ingredients and spices; the main differences between the two culinary cousins lies in the distinctive accompanying *achar* in Nepal, and chilli oil or soy sauce in China. On a further East and South Asian culinary note, *Chow Chow* (Chow Mein) is a very popular dish in Nepal, where it is usually accompanied by either a tomato sauce or a spicy green sauce.

When ordering meat, you should be aware that Nepalis do not section carcasses into the joints and cuts typical in the West. Instead, slices are carved and then chopped into small pieces to be eaten on the bone. Meat can often contain bone splinters and gristle, so look out for this, or ask for "boneless" meat.

Outside tourist areas, *daal bhat* is likely to be what is available, although some better restaurants in urban centers may offer a few Indian dishes. If, after a week's trekking, you feel the need for greater variety, restaurants in Kathmandu and Pokhara offer an incredible range of different types of food, from a full English breakfast to Chinese, Italian, Mexican, Tibetan, Japanese, French, or Russian specialties.

When ordering, remember that food is likely to be cooked very fresh—the chicken may still be flapping around when you place the order. There may well be just one cook producing everything. If everyone orders something different you may sit there for a very long time. That said, eating is not just a matter of face feeding and accessing nutrition; it is a major part of Nepali culture and daily life. Nepali chefs in the West have a well-deserved high reputation for their cooking.

Nepalis commonly drink water (*paani*) with their meal. Always make sure to drink bottled water (with the plastic wrapping intact at the opening/top), or to check that the water has been boiled.

International brands of fizzy drinks are bottled in Nepal and several breweries produce Nepali beer. *Raksi* (distilled from rice), *chhaang* (Nepali and Tibetan beer), and related to the latter *tongba* (the fermented millet drink, drunk through a straw out of a bamboo flagon) may also be available, and Nepali whiskey (such as Signature) is an option too.

Tea (*chiya*), usually made with milk (*dudh*), is available everywhere. Coffee, although grown in Nepal for export, is generally only available in the tourist areas. As dishes are generally left to drip-dry, you should also ensure plates and glasses are dry before using them.

Wherever you choose to eat out in Nepal, people are friendly and eager to please. If traveling with children you may even find it liberating: where else will a waiter take the time to build paper airplanes with your son, fold lotus flowers out of serviettes for your daughter, or carry your baby around while you eat in peace?

TIPPING

Tipping is common and expected by waiters, cleaners, and luggage porters in restaurants and hotels in tourist areas. Tips constitute a significant proportion of the earnings of porter-guides in the mountains. For cleaners and porters at airports, some loose change is sufficient. In expensive restaurants you should tip up to 10 percent. This is also appropriate for porter-guides. Tipping is not expected in self-service restaurants, and, while not required, is welcomed by taxi and rickshaw drivers when paying the agreed fare at end of your journey.

CROWDS AND FINDING SPACE

"Privacy" is not even a concept in this collective society. The word does not exist in the Nepali language. The nature of Nepali life means that much activity is conducted in the open. You can have your hair cut outside, medical treatment may be administered at the pharmacist's counter, a tailor may measure you for new clothes on the street. You may also find yourself trying to make an international telephone call in an open-fronted shop, where noise from the road outside is likely to be a far greater problem than any worries about confidentiality—the same applies to Internet calls from Internet cafés (although the wide use of cell phones for such calls provides more options for

Al fresco haircut in Kathmandu.

privacy). Protecting what you consider to be "your own space" can be difficult, especially when you may be regarded as an exotic species! Complete strangers may walk into your house uninvited, their only pretext to see how you live. Similarly, you can expect an audience on any shopping excursion outside tourist areas.

Your shopping at local markets will often be as much fun for your audience as it is for you. Unless you know the correct word for *uncooked* rice, the fun begins when you try to buy some. There are numerous different words meaning rice in Nepali, and a pulses and cereals shop will have various sacks for you to choose from. You might think you are doing well to remember *daal bhat* and ask for "bhat," but this will just get you a grin—and maybe an invitation to sit down for a plate of cooked/boiled rice (which is what *bhat* is). To purchase *uncooked* rice in shops, ask for *chamal.* Rice growing in the paddy field has a different name, *dhaan.*

Laughter is the Spice of Life

I caused hilarity in the market one day when I tried to buy a selection of spices—usually sold by the kilogram in Nepal, which was the problem, as I was looking for the sort of quantity you would find in a Western supermarket, which is probably nearer 50 g (1.76 oz). I tried telling them we only planned to stay for two years, but that just made them laugh all the more.

You may not always enjoy the constant entourage, but at least you are never likely to feel threatened personally by crowds in Nepal. Nor will you be constantly hassled by persistent beggars.

SINGING—THE ROLE OF SONG AND MUSIC IN DAILY LIFE

You will soon become aware that music and song are ever-present in Kathmandu, almost everywhere. People sing when on their own, in formal, community settings such as traditional dance festivals, and at private family events. Nepali music is generally speaking vibrant and cheerful. Traditional Nepali instrumental music— played on the *sitar*, *tabla*, and the *bansuri*, or Nepali

Sita Maiya Rajchal in concert.

flute—is regarded as being of great quality and purity, and is very widely enjoyed. The Nepalis are rightly proud of their musical heritage, and there are many musical contests at national level; in 2019 Sita Maiya Rajchal, a member of the Government of Nepal Music Board, won a World Book of Records title for standing *sitar* playing. Do not leave Nepal without acquainting yourself with the depth, breadth, and richness of Nepali traditional music, and indeed contemporary popular song.

SHOPPING FOR PLEASURE

It is possible to buy almost anything in Kathmandu. A wide range of imported produce and merchandise is on offer, from beef—not an everyday commodity in a Hindu country—to the latest in digital cameras, cell phones, and the like. Visitors are most likely to be interested in the vast range of traditional and ethnic Nepali arts and handicrafts, production of which is concentrated in the Kathmandu valley, but which are found of course throughout the country.

Hand-knotted carpets are produced by Tibetans at the refugee camp in Jawalakhel on the edge of Patan, or around the Buddhist *stupa* at Bodhnath. Here you will also find Tibetan clothing, prayer wheels, and other Buddhist ornaments. Colorful *thangka* paintings, typically depicting the Wheel of Life, are available at Bodhnath, in Bhaktapur, or around Kathmandu's Durbar Square. Their quality and price depend upon the talent and experience of the artist.

Jewelry can be purchased "off the shelf," or created for you with loose gems selected in the shops in the bustling neighborhood of Thamel or in New Road. You can watch paper products being handmade in Thamel and Bhaktapur. Thimi, between Kathmandu and Bhaktapur, is famous for its papier mâché masks and puppets. Potters display their craft and wares at Potters' Square in Bhaktapur. Highly skilled Newar craftsmen still have workshops in Bhaktapur and Patan, producing traditional wood carvings and engraved copper, brass, and bronze items.

In Thamel you can buy traditional *khukuri* knives, made famous by the Gurkhas, or have your clothes embroidered with a motif of your choice or design. Pashmina wool from the inner coat of Himalayan goats (better known as cashmere) is woven into luxury shawls and other garments on hand looms in the valley and represents one of the country's fastest growing exports.

In most places you will be expected to bargain, but this is all part of the fun. A few words of Nepali may give you a completely different basis for negotiation. Be careful not to insult anyone by pitching your first offer too low. Aim to pay around 20 percent under the asking price.

Very little of what is on sale is old, although unscrupulous traders may try to convince you that you are buying a valuable antique. If something looks genuinely old, ask the shop to provide a receipt. It is forbidden to export antiques. Antique hunters are advised to bring a Nepali friend with them on antique purchasing forays, as the purchase may require formal approval for export by the Department of Archaeology in Kathmandu, which will issue a permit to wave at customs as you leave.

If you dislike bargaining, or wish to get a feel for what things should cost, there are a few shops in Kathmandu that sell fairly priced goods produced by development projects supporting low-income groups. Ask a taxi driver for "Dhukuti," "Mahaguthi," or "Folk Nepal." The Women's Foundation offers a refuge to displaced women and trains them in such skills as weaving. The pashminas and other woven shawls they produce fund the refuge.

CULTURAL AND SOCIAL LIFE

People generally tended to retire and rise with the sun, especially in rural and remote areas. However in recent years, with the end of electricity "load-shedding," this pattern, especially in Kathmandu, has been changing.

A Night-in

In domestic settings, watching TV is a major source of entertainment and a social focus. This takes place exclusively within the context of family, or family and friends, and in private homes. In some cases, once the bonds of friendship have been established, you may be invited to Nepali homes where the TV will form part of the entertainment, over tea, or stronger drinks and snacks, or a Nepali meal. TV programs include news, talent and challenges/endurance test shows (local equivalents of the UK's "X Factor" and "Big Brother" and "I'm a Celebrity get me Out of Here"), films, and serials, many of which are from India as well as Nepal.

Visiting the Zoo

Kathmandu Central Zoo is visited by more than a
million people each year and is a "family day out"
institution, well worth visiting if you want to touch
base with authentic Nepali Kathmandu.

Through the work of a British national, Paul Nash,
and the UK Nepal Friendship Society, the zoo has
been transformed and brought up to international
standards on animal welfare, with other improvements
such as clear well-written information in English. The
experience it offers helps raise awareness of many of
Nepal's native species, such as the Red Panda, the Bengal
tiger, and others. It also includes an animal rescue
unit, not open to the general public but accessible if
permission is applied for. Here you can sometimes find
man-eating tigers, as in Nepal dangerous animals are
only put down in rare and extreme circumstances. Many
of the animals in the zoo (such as the monkey, buffalo,
tiger, or snake) have religious and spiritual associations
with Nepali and broader South Asian deities.

The Performing Arts

Understandably you will not find much Western "high
culture" here. Nepal's own diverse and rich heritage finds
expression in its folklore, epic tales, and religious fables
passed down by word of mouth or enacted in colorful
pageants of song and dance.

Traditional dance and music are popular and reflect
the religious, cultural, and personal experiences of
the Nepali people. They are an integral part of the
performance of Sanskrit epics, and many religious

festivals involve dancing at the temple. People will dance at home, and traditional songs and dances form part of any school concert. Dance performances are often provided for tourists. Though this on the one hand represents a commercialization of Nepalese culture and music, it has also helped preserve folk arts by providing an income for the performers.

Theater is highly regarded in Nepal, and a visit to the contemporary Mandala Theatre, in Anamnagar in the Singha Durbar district of Kathmandu, is a must for theater lovers. Conventional theater with its formal stage settings has been used in Hindu and Buddhist cultures and religious rites for centuries.

Traditional dance-dramas commonly relate the stories of religious and national heroes. There are masked performances, and regionally distinct folk theater performances. Before the passing of the 2015 Constitution, and particularly toward the end of the monarchy, street theater was used very effectively to advocate democratic values and rights, as well as to raise awareness on women's, children's, and minority social issues—ethnic, lower caste/Dalits, but others too.

For the musical arts, venues in Thamel, Kathmandu, provide platforms where some of Nepal's finest talents, such Sita Maiya Rajchal, regularly perform.

Cinema

Cinema is second only to television in popularity. Until recently men and women would sit on different sides of the auditorium to watch films, but this practice and requirement has largely disappeared. The program

Poster of the movie *American Babu Made in Nepal.*

tends to be dominated by Bollywood movies, shown in Hindi, occasionally with English subtitles. Hindi is quite closely related to Nepali and widely understood in Nepal.

Nepal's own high-quality film industry is disproportionately influential in South Asia. In its infancy it had considerable help from the Indian film industry and saw the introduction of a still important Bollywood influence. However, it would be a mistake to see contemporary Nepali film as a shadow of its more famous neighbor to the south.

Over the past thirty years Nepal's film industry has grown and evolved. The old so called *masala* genre—a cocktail of spices, usually a variation on the themes of love and betrayal, with lots of violence and melodramatic music thrown in—continues to exist, but alongside different types of film and subjects. These include subtle, contemporary productions where human psychology or existential themes dominate, and generic drama and suspense films for the international market. The crime action movie *Loot* (2012), about five ordinary men who band together to improve their fortunes by robbing a bank, and the searing social commentary of *Pashupati Prasad* (2016), are examples of award-winning films that match the best of Indian and global cinematography. Both have subtitles and are easily accessible to English-speaking audiences.

In fact, Nepali acting talent has had a significant impact in India and is evident in that country's TV talent dance and singing contests and shows. Not far behind in this are the Nepali film make-up artists, fashion designers, and models who make contributions in their respective fields in Bollywood and beyond.

Fashion

Kathmandu also has an internationally respected fashion industry, and an accompanying modeling world, with talent not only being sought from and making its way to Mumbai and New Delhi, but increasingly to the West. One of the world's top fashion designers, New York-based Prabal Gurung, is Nepali, and North American and European fashion designers are tapping in to the huge reserve of high-end tailoring skill found in Nepal's capital, even to the extent of establishing factories there. The economic opportunities being developed here will have the effect of harnessing and retaining this talent in Nepal.

Galleries

There are several art galleries in Kathmandu exhibiting both historical and contemporary works. The Nepal Art Council (Nepal's official national gallery, in Madan Bhandari Road, Singha Durbar), Siddhartha Art Gallery (in Babermahal Revisited, Singha Durbar), and Bikalpa Arts Center (in Pulchowk, in Lalitpur/Patan) are three particularly important ones.

Ordinary Nepalis are surrounded by beautiful ancient religious art, particularly sculptures, every day of their lives in temples, *stupas*, streets, and town squares. The Maithili and Tharu peoples of the Terai decorate the adobe walls of their houses with murals, drawing on folklore and religion as themes. Women's empowerment and equality charities, such as the Janakpur-based Janaki Women Awareness Society (JWAS), generate income to support those they care for and for campaigning work and projects, by selling distinctive high-quality ethnic "Mithila" artworks (paintings and craft items) created by their members. Similarly, the Special School and Development Centre (SSDRC)—a dedicated support center for those with autism and their carers, led by the deeply respected Sabita Upreti—sells high-end Nepali clothing and items such as scarves of great beauty, often in international styles, created by SSDRC members.

These examples are part of a growing phenomenon— the preservation of Nepal's ancient cultures by fostering its arts and crafts and sharing these with the world. Hand-made works such as scroll paintings or modern pieces using ancient motifs can be bought locally or in Kathmandu

Literature

The best bookstores are located in Thamel. Two in particular are worth a mention. Pilgrims Book House is a good starting point to investigate Nepali literature. Folktales, legends, and children's stories are available in translation and show the origins of many Nepali beliefs, customs, traditions, and inhibitions. Some renowned Nepali writers have also produced works in English. These include collections of short stories and essays on current issues that give invaluable insights into contemporary Nepali society.

Vajra Books, in the Jyatha quarter, is owned by the knowledgeable Bidur Dangol. While it also stocks tourist guides, it specializes in more academic books. This is a great place to come if you need something on the anthropology of Nepali hill tribes or want to read up on Newari architecture. Vajra is more than just a bookstore and publisher. The remarkable thing about this place is that "if you buy a book here, you may well meet the author as well." Nepali journalists and academics drop in regularly, as do experts from abroad in everything from economic development to Buddhism.

SPORTS

Nepal is not a nation of sports fanatics, but this is to some extent changing. Two sports are particularly popular, football (soccer) and volleyball, although cricket enjoys popularity too. Plains dwellers will say it is too hot, while those in the mountains have no need for any further cardiovascular expansion! Modesty requirements further restrict women. The results of Asian sports competitions are, however, enthusiastically reported in the press, and events such as the football World Cup draw television spectators despite the country's nonparticipation. Expats living in Kathmandu may have occasion to play football or cricket against other organizations or school groups, and there are elite sports and golf clubs in Kathmandu and Pokhara.

Discussions are under way for a friendly international football match to take place in 2021 between the Nepal national team and the England C team, under the aegis of the English Football Association and the All Nepal Football Association. A Nepali initiative by the UK Nepal Friendship Society to support of the Sahara UK organization (the British Nepali community organization involved in promoting football), this will give a major boost to the profile of the game, which is enjoyed in Nepal with great passion but ever acrimony.

Around Dashain, after the monsoon when the air is fresh and winds are high, the Nepali sport of choice is kite flying. Thousands of kites take to the skies at this time—some as primitive as plastic bags on strings, others far more elaborate. This sport is highly competitive, as the object is to drive nearby kites out of the sky. Also at this time of year, huge swings are built from fresh, supple bamboo poles lashed together with rope, as one of the activities related Dashain.

THE GREAT OUTDOORS

Nepal's appeal for most visitors is, of course, its unique landscape, which offers some of the finest trekking in the world, the ultimate in mountaineering, spectacular and arduous mountain biking routes, and the dramatic thrills of white-water rafting down some of the world's deepest, steepest gorges.

Trekking

Most of Nepal can still only be accessed on foot, and trekking is thus the only way to visit remote communities. The most popular routes are the trek to the Everest base camp, those in the Helambu and Langtang valleys north of Kathmandu, and those in the Annapurna region near Pokhara. The advantage of trekking in these regions is that there are lodges offering food and accommodation at frequent intervals along the way, so that it is possible to trek independently, even with children. If you want to trek off the beaten path, you will have to be quite self-sufficient.

Lodges on the main routes are simple, generally clean, and inexpensive, although food and drinks become more expensive with increasing altitude (someone has to carry it all up there). Facilities are shared. Staff in lodges usually speak some English, but an English-speaking porter-guide can be arranged through your hotel in Pokhara or a reputable agency. They walk with you, recommend lodges, and are happy to fill you in on cultural details or quirks of the

The view from High Camp on the Annapurna circuit.

mountains as you trek. On the main trekking routes permits to enter the National Parks are required. Permits are also required for trekking in more remote areas.

Mountaineering

Eight out of ten of the world's highest mountains are in Nepal. You can only climb them as part of an official expedition. As a result of the devastation caused by large expeditions felling trees for firewood and abandoning all sorts of mountaineering equipment, Nepal's government now restricts the number of expeditions and charges fees, which have become an important source of hard currency for the country.

Mount Everest (Sagarmartha) has in recent years become a giant repository of rubbish left by trekkers and climbers. Since 2014, mountaineers and trekkers have been required on their return to take back rubbish of up to 8 kilos (17.64 pounds) in weight—the amount the government estimates an exhausted climber discards *en route*.

One doesn't have to be a mountaineer though to enjoy the Himalayas, as the mountains can be seen in all their panoramic splendor in most parts of the country, and can be approached by much less arduous trekking in their foothills, and by special air flights.

Mountain Biking

Mountain bikes can be rented in Kathmandu. This is one of the best ways to visit out-of-the-way temples, *stupas*, and villages. The Tribhuvan Highway from Kathmandu to Hetauda has a grueling 13,123 ft. (4,000 m) ascent, but the reward is an incomparable view of Himalayan peaks from a viewing point at Daman, followed by a dramatic descent through rhododendron forests.

Bungee Jumping

Nepal's terrain was made for bungee jumping , which has become a major attraction. Suspension bridges over ravines and canyons are common locations, with spectacular mountain views and panoramas amplifying the experience. World-leading bungee consultants have been heavily involved in developing the sport, and new locations are being opened up across the country.

White-water Rafting

Depending on the season, Nepal's rivers rage or meander through lush green valleys and deep gorges, offering exceptional rafting opportunities for both beginners and the more experienced. The most popular river is the easily accessible Trishuli, which can take you from west of Kathmandu all the way down to Chitwan National Park. You are likely to see more white water and wildlife on other, more remote rivers, however.

Chitwan National Park

No trip to Nepal would be complete without a visit to the Chitwan National Park, an extensive area of subtropical lowlands (about 370 sq. mi./958 sq. km) covering parts of the Nawalpur, Parsa, Chitwan, and Makwanpur districts of south-central Nepal. The park was established in 1973 and in 1984 gained World Heritage Site status thanks to its exceptional wildlife and natural environment.

Chitwan's iconic elephant safaris are a thrilling way to explore the jungle. You may spot wild rhinos, deer,

peacocks, and crocodiles. Tigers are more elusive, but this endangered species benefits from the park's protection. In some cases villages have even been relocated to help their habitat. To the immediate east of the reserve is Parsa National Park, which connects to the south with the Tiger Reserve of Valmiki National Park in India.

The gateway to Chitwan National Park is the former village of Sauraha, grown to the dimensions of a town with numerous hotels, yet still retaining many aspects of its original village life.

CHAPTER SEVEN

TRAVEL, HEALTH, & SAFETY

ARRIVING

Most visitors arriving in Nepal land at the country's only international airport, Kathmandu's Tribhuvan International Airport. There are three main overland routes from India, and one from Tibet. Drivers must have an international carnet. They must also leave the country again with their vehicles or face astronomical import duties. Buses operate on all four routes.

The cool polished floors and unhurried lines of Tribhuvan's modern, air-conditioned international terminal may surprise you. They certainly do little to prepare you for the colorfulness and bustle of the capital city outside! Only traveling passengers are permitted to enter the building.

It is possible to enter Nepal without a visa, which can be purchased and completed in the arrivals area before you clear passport control. Visas are generated by machines in the hall and there can be lines; you also need to pay an accompanying entry fee before

Entering the melée outside Tribhuvan International Airport.

proceeding to immigration control (all in the same area). Once you have passed through security, you enter the baggage reclaim area on the ground floor; space is tight and it can be a scramble around the luggage carousels.

If you are being picked up, you may be met with a *khada* (a ceremonial scarf, often of silk or satin), or garlands of flowers—a special honor for "auspicious guests." Independent travelers can best reach the city center by taxi. These generally have black license plates and will be waiting outside. Some drivers may try to take you to a hotel they know, so be clear about what you want and where you have booked to stay. For trips from the airport to locations within the beltway, known here as the "ring-road," there is normally a fixed rate.

URBAN TRANSPORTATION

When you exit the airport on to the main road into the city, calm gives way to frenetic tumult and chaos. All of a sudden you will find yourself part of a teeming mass of taxis, cars, buses, trucks, auto-rickshaws, bicycle rickshaws, motorcycles, three-wheeled tempo "buses," pedestrians, bicycles, to say nothing of holy cows nonchalantly chewing the cud in the middle of it all. There is definitely a charm to all this noisy activity, the bustle of real life in motion.

Traffic is both noisy and generally very polluting, but this probably has more to do with the age and efficiency of the vehicles than with speed. The origins of Kathmandu's pollution problem lie in its unplanned population expansion, the growing wealth of many more people (meaning more disposable income being spent on buying cars), and the fact that most vehicles come from neighboring India where the tightening up of anti-pollution laws meant that vehicles that no longer met the requirements in India itself could still find a market in Nepal. Happily the situation is changing as a combination of Nepali legislation and anti-pollution campaigns, are starting to have an impact.

The congestion means that nothing actually moves very fast on the busier routes, but on Kathmandu's newly created multilane (in some cases four to each direction of travel!) ring-road you will be delighted by the ease of travel and space. The chaos results from the volume of traffic and, to Western eyes at least, an apparent lack of adherence to any formal highway code. Officially people drive on the left. Many drivers are not properly trained, licensed, or insured. There used to be few sidewalks outside Kathmandu, and very few in Thamel, the tourist hub of the capital. This picture is though changing.

Private Vehicles

Until a few years ago, mainly due to prohibitive import taxes even on old cars, very few Nepalis owned a car, and the vehicle of choice for middle-class families was a motorbike. Among wealthy families, a motorbike is also a typical wedding present for a son-in-law. There is nothing unusual in seeing a motorcyclist taking his wife to the market, and dropping off a couple of children at school on the way. You may even see a goat riding pillion on the way home! However, with the rise in prosperity the number of cars on the roads has grown exponentially, particularly all-terrain four-wheel drive vehicles popular with wealthier Nepalis due to the challenges of some of Kathmandu's road surfaces, and for those traveling outside the capital. Otherwise people still continue to use public transportation in large numbers.

Taxis

Taxis are largely confined to Kathmandu and Pokhara. Make sure the meter is switched on before you set off, or negotiate a price for your journey in advance. Hiring a taxi for the day is arguably the best way to explore the Kathmandu valley and, particularly if there are a few of you, it is not expensive. If you need a taxi outside the

Kathmandu and Pokhara areas, ask around—a local hotel will normally arrange a car for you.

Thuk-thuks, Rickshaws, and Bicycles

Few towns in Nepal are big enough to warrant city buses. Instead there are *thuk-thuks*. These auto-rickshaws, also known as *tempos*, are spluttering, three-wheeled scooters. The smaller ones carry two or three passengers, tend to be metered, and operate much as taxis do, although they are far less comfortable. The bigger ones are designed for eight to ten people, may well carry fifteen, and operate on fixed routes, with each passenger paying a few rupees to the boy hanging on at the back. They can be useful for short distances, but the problem for tourists is how to recognize where they are going.

Public transportation in Chitwan.

Bicycle rickshaws are common in the old part of Kathmandu and in towns in the Terai. They are slow and bumpy, but can be useful for short distances through crowded, narrow streets, or if you don't want to walk in the dusty heat. Find out what fare is expected before you set off; you will be charged more in tourist areas.

Bicycles are an ideal way of navigating small towns. Smog and chaotic traffic are hazards in Kathmandu.

GETTING AROUND THE COUNTRY

Any long-distance journey in Nepal is likely to be something of an adventure. Distances are not huge, but delays are frequent and progress slow due to the terrain. Although Nepal's territory is small in extent, it includes many of the world's highest mountain peaks and, with the exception of the Terai in the borderlands with India, most of the country is mountainous, and consequently routes from A to B are necessarily circuitous. Some of the most dramatic scenery in the world goes a long way toward compensating for any discomfort, and you will rarely make a journey without collecting an enduring memory of some cameo of Nepali life.

With just one 30-mile (48-km) stretch of railway from Janakpur in the Terai to Jaynagar in India, the majority of travelers stick to a standard itinerary of destinations on roads in the middle of the country. Prior to the mid-2010s, Nepal's road network was one of the least developed in the world. This has changed considerably.

The first road to connect Kathmandu with the outside world was the Tribhuvan Highway, built by the

Indian government in the 1950s. A considerable feat of engineering, this winds south over the mountains from the Prithvi Highway at Naubise to Hetauda, and on to the Indian border at Birgunj. The tortuous 67 miles (107 km) from Naubise to Hetauda are worth it for the views, but it still takes about six hours by car.

Outside the capital until recently only the Mahendra Highway was consistently wide enough for buses to pass without slowing down. On narrow stretches of road smaller vehicles give way to larger ones for reasons of self-preservation! Maintenance of the highways can be irregular (this, too, is improving) and, especially during and just after the monsoon, landslides frequently render roads impassable, causing huge delays. The Tribhuvan Highway may also be closed in winter due to snow.

Buses

Bus stations, which can seem chaotic to new eyes, are important hubs of daily life for many Nepalis, with vendors milling around offering bottled water and snacks to eat on your journey. Destinations are not always written in English, so you may have to ask for help. Buses are well used, so it is better to buy your ticket a day in advance. If staying in Kathmandu or Pokhara, you can ask your hotel to arrange for tickets.

Private and state bus companies operate along all paved roads in Nepal. Buses are cheap. That said, they also have a reputation for being generally uncomfortable, crowded, noisy, sometimes dirty, slow, and prone to overheating and breakdown. They may have suicidally high centers of gravity due to the number of passengers, goats, suitcases, and sofas perched on the roof. As drivers sometimes also give the impression that they are relying a little too much on *karma*, you should be prepared for a thrilling ride. Reports of buses leaving the road to plunge into a gorge are rare.

Journeys used to be delayed, before 2015, by multiple police and army checks that entailed everyone alighting to walk through a checkpoint (foreigners sometimes excepted), not to mention various tea and *daal bhat* stops at the driver's discretion. These refreshment stops in fact provide valuable rest and socialization opportunities, amid, as is the case almost anywhere in Nepal, majestic natural surroundings.

Greenline tourist buses (http://greenline.com.np) are recommended for foreign visitors traveling between Kathmandu, Pokhara, and Chitwan. They are cleaner

On the Araniko Highway between Kathmandu and the border crossing with Tibet.

and better maintained, tend to be driven more carefully, and stop only at Greenline stations, where the facilities are clean and a *daal bhat* buffet is included in the price of your ticket, which also applies to other higher-end international-travel coach businesses in Nepal.

Car and Bike Rental

It is not generally possible to rent a car and drive it yourself in Nepal. Instead, you hire one with a driver. This has advantages. A driver will know where to find gas, and where he can leave the car. He is also used to the peculiarities of Nepal's highways. And if the worst comes to the worst and you do have an accident, it could save you a lot of hassle. If you arrange for a driver outside Kathmandu to take you to the capital, you should be aware that he is only permitted to take you as far as the beltway. City taxis have exclusive licenses for the area within the "ring road."

Motorbikes can be hired in Kathmandu and are a versatile way of seeing the country: they can usually be pushed around craters in the road. Beware of the drops in temperature that come with altitude and be sure to pack a scarf and gloves, and for motorbike travel in the Terai, plenty of sealed-bottled, safe-to-use water.

Flying

Aircraft are a crucial component of the transportation infrastructure, especially in the far west, where they are used to airlift food supplies in winter. Until recently, some airstrips were a days' walk from the nearest road. Nepal Airlines and several private airlines operate small propeller aircraft between various towns. Most flights start or end in Kathmandu.

In clear conditions a domestic flight can be a fascinating experience, and it certainly saves a lot of time. Flights are, however, often disrupted by fog or other poor weather conditions. Domestic airports are fairly basic, so make sure you have something to eat and drink with you in case your flight is delayed.

Visitors are expected to pay for flights mostly in hard currency, and pay a higher rate. Porters are available to carry your luggage to or from your taxi or bus in return for a small tip (agree the amount beforehand).

WHERE TO STAY

In the Kathmandu valley, Pokhara, and around Chitwan National Park you will find all grades of accommodation, from basic budget hostels to five-star hotels with swimming pools. In the past these options were limited to just those three locations, but today there are many more destinations in Nepal offering a range of possibilities. If traveling independently you can often negotiate a good price on the spot for a pleasant room including a private bathroom, hot water, and breakfast. People will go out of their way to be helpful and arrange for anything else you need.

In bigger towns in the Terai a range of standards of accommodation may be available, with growing choice at the top end, too. Bear in mind that it can get very hot here, and that mosquitoes can be a problem. Look for rooms with fans and mosquito nets as a minimum.

Lodges on major trekking routes are plentiful, simple to middle-range comfortable, and adequate. Here it is advisable to take your own sleeping bag.

Away from the major tourist haunts and urban centers accommodation often used to be quite primitive However, the situation is changing rapidly as a consequence of a strategic initiative to attract wealthy, educated tourists who come to Nepal, not to climb mountains or go trekking, but for spiritual and wellbeing reasons, seeking a deeper cultural experience from their visit. As a result there has been a focus on improving the level of hygiene (in kitchens and restrooms especially) and comfort for international visitors, and of course for Nepal's own burgeoning middle class.

It is possible to stay with local families. The accommodation is not likely to be luxurious, but you will be warmly received and the experience will give you a fascinating insight into the Nepali way of life.

HEALTH AND SAFETY

Medical and health care in Nepal presents a contrasting picture in both quality and levels of access, with the gap narrowing in recent years. There are no obligatory vaccinations for visitors, but you should ensure all basic vaccinations are up to date, and check current recommendations for other appropriate vaccinations with your embassy or the Ciwec Clinic Travel Medicine

Center in Kathmandu before you travel. There are incidences of both Japanese encephalitis and malaria in Nepal. Whether you need vaccinations or prophylactic medication will depend on where you will be spending time. Rabies vaccinations are a consideration if traveling to remote areas because of the time needed to get back to civilization in the event of being bitten. It may also be necessary to take precautions against hepatitis, typhoid, and meningitis. Tuberculosis used to be endemic in some parts of Nepal, but the risk to travelers is low unless you are going to spend lots of time with lots of people in enclosed places.

For longer stays in remote country districts, a good basic health care manual, such as *Where There Is No Doctor—A Village Health Care Handbook* by David Werner, is recommended, not only for your personal use but because you may also be asked for advice. It can be helpful to talk to locals, as they sometimes recognize symptoms you may not have encountered before.

There are some good clinics in Kathmandu, Pokhara, and more recently in Chitwan. Health facilities in most other locations are poor or non-existent. Medical treatment at Western travelers' clinics is expensive. Comprehensive travel and health insurance is essential.

Many medicines are readily available at pharmacies, with or without prescriptions, and in many cases are much cheaper than they would be in the West. Especially in mountain regions, it is safer to have a supply of antiseptics and antibiotics with you than to rely on finding them. You would also be removing them from the very scanty stocks of remote mountain outposts.

If you do have to seek help, doctors will speak English. Other staff may not. In the event of admission to hospital, it is as well to know that relatives and friends are normally expected to bring in all food and be on hand to run errands, such as going to the hospital pharmacy to purchase any medicines, anesthetics, or items of equipment that may be needed. In terms of timely personal care, from nurses to doctors and consultants, private hospitals in Nepal are exceptionally good.

Dental Care

Private dental care in Nepal is well established and has been consolidated in recent years with a very good reputation for dental-care tourism. The quality and affordability of Nepal's private sector dentistry is well known to British diplomats and related circles!

Water and Dairy Products

If accidents are the biggest single risk to the lives of visitors to Nepal, the biggest potential health risk is undoubtedly the water. In many places sewers are open, even if in recent years the situation has been improving. In remote rural areas the following conditions are still not uncommon. Sewage and water pipes often leak and may be one above the other. You can catch amoebic dysentery, typhoid, diarrhea, hepatitis, bacterial infections, worms, and other parasites, so never: drink from a faucet, accept water to drink if you are not certain it has been both boiled and filtered, eat fruit you have not peeled or washed yourself in safe water, brush your teeth with the water, or sing in the shower! Parts of some rivers can be polluted with refuse—floating, sunk, swimming, or, in the case of the cadavers, bouncing along bloated. There have been improvements in the Bagmati River, which runs through the capital and through the sacred Pashupatinath Temple, through "Clean up the Bagmati" campaigns.

Milk and other dairy products can also be a problem. Milk should be boiled, even if the bag does say "pasteurized." Bhaktapur is famous for its delicious yogurt (*dhau*), but you should always scrape the top off, as it is left to set in open bowls in the sun, often at the roadside.

NATURAL HAZARDS

Altitude

Altitude sickness can and does kill. To avoid it, ascend slowly and give yourself plenty of time to acclimatize. If symptoms of nausea, tiredness, and severe headaches persist, you should return to a lower altitude and seek medical advice.

Don't stand on the valley side of a path to let a mule train pass!

Flooding and Landslides

Road conditions are poor at the best of times in Nepal, but the arrival of the monsoon can turn trickling streams into raging torrents capable of tearing away bridges and transporting rocks the size of houses miles downstream. Flooding and frequent landslides render many roads impassable and cut off remote regions. Climate change is exacerbating these perennial challenges.

Climate Change and Nepal

Climate change is hitting the Himalayas very hard, resulting in melting glaciers, an unprecedented raising of the treeline, and the drying up of springs and watercourses that used to sustain vibrant agricultural communities. In many locations in Nepal, such as Sindhupalchowk district in the zone below the High Himalayas, the terraces have become wildernesses and communities are on the point of extinction due to climatic instability. Long periods of aridity, unseasonable intense rainfall, including life-threatening flash floods, and shifting patterns of snowfall and of heat and cold, are causing major disruption and accelerating the flight from the land to urban areas. The destruction of the ecosystem and its associated forms of agriculture means that traditional cultures are being lost as people reestablish their lives in alien, urban settings.

Diversification away from traditional agriculture to other wealth creating activities, such as Rainbow Trout farming, and support for the tourism sector in opening up trekking, is providing some relief from the effects of climate change, and imaginative solutions are emerging, such as micro-hydropower projects at village level to provide both power and irrigation. So this is a changing scenario and a positive one. Nepal is a world leader in raising awareness of the impact of climate change.

Earthquakes (*Bhukamp*)

Nepal is situated on one of the world's major tectonic fault lines. Its worst recent earthquake was April 25, 2015 in the Gorkha area, measuring 7.9 on the Richter Scale. A further earthquake took place in June of that year, and the combined fatalities were 9,000. Experts believed that another major earthquake was overdue, since the preceding major earthquake to hit the country was in 1934, when it is believed that 20,000 people were killed

Earth tremors are common in this region and may also cause landslides and avalanches. "Earthquake kits" are available in some tourist shops. They include bottled water, canned food, and a spade. Some hotels in Kathmandu provide information on how to behave in the event of an earthquake—it is as well to read it.

CRIME

As in any big city, you should be on your guard against pickpockets in the bustle of Kathmandu, particularly in Thamel, and lesser tourist destinations. The country no doubt also has its share of swindlers plying dubious wares. Crime levels, however, are exceptionally low compared with other parts of the world. No racism, violent robbery, anti-social behavior, stabbings, acid attacks, or terrorist incidents have been reported in Nepal. Even at the height of the Maoist insurgency a decade ago the insurgents did all in their power to avoid involving international visitors in the conflict out of respect for Nepal's good name internationally, evidence of the Nepali value of respect for the stranger and the concept of "Guest is God." As regards crime, unless there is an extremely rare exception, nothing worse is likely to happen to you than a half-eaten biscuit being swiped from your hand by a monkey at Swayambunath!

There have been reports of trekkers being robbed, but this is not common. As anywhere, you should stick to the main routes. Do not trek alone, not because of robbers but because there are still wild tigers to be found in the remoter parts of Nepal's stunning countryside.

DON'T MISS

A Walk Through Old Kathmandu

Take a walk through the teeming lanes between Durbar Square and Thamel and allow your senses to be assailed by the vibrant colors of women's saris, gaudy shop fronts, powder-smeared shrines, the scents of incense and spices, and the cacophony of horns, bells, and tradesmen's calls. The textile shops often have skilled tailors on hand (*Master ji*) who can run up bespoke clothes to traditional Nepali or Western designs. Craft shops hold a multitude of treasures. Brass and copper ware, Buddhist and Hindu religious icons, and fabric patterns have ancient origins, and are a living continuation of cultures from very early times.

Bhaktapur

Wander through the brick-paved alleys of this perfectly preserved Newari medieval city, a UNESCO World Heritage site, with its temples, pagoda roofs, and elaborate carvings. Bhaktapur (also known in

Pottery Square in Bhaktapur.

Nepal as "Khwopa") is cleaner than Kathmandu and
traffic is largely banned from its center. Its name
"Bhaktapur" means "The place of devotees." During
the Malla Dynasty, Bhaktapur was the largest of the
three Newari kingdoms of the Kathmandu valley, and
was the capital city of Nepal in the second half of the
fifteenth century. Bhaktapur is nationally famous for
a particular form of yogurt (generically, *Dahi*) known
as "Ju Ju Dhau" (in the Newari language, also known
as Nepal Bhasa, "King's Curd"). It suffered substantial
damage in the 2015 earthquakes, but its exceptional
medieval architecture survived largely unscathed, and
its quiet charm, compared to Kathmandu eight miles
away, never fails to captivate. Its monumental squares,
streets, sacred and domestic architecture, wood,
brick and stonework are a living paradise for artists,
photographers, and lovers of history and architecture.

The great prayer bell at Bodhnath.

Bodhnath

Circumambulate this oasis of calm in the hubbub of Kathmandu and discover its history and special associations with Tibetan Buddhism. This giant *stupa* in the northeast of the city, one of the largest in the world and a UNESCO World Heritage Site, is one of its main landmarks. Its architecture is stunning and its circular perimeter is lined with inward-facing buildings of great beauty, including homes and shops.

Bodhnath is situated on an ancient trade route from Tibet. Since the late 1950s Tibetan Buddhists have settled here in considerable numbers, establishing more than fifty convents (*gombas*). It is said that the *stupa* itself contains the remains of the Kassapa Buddha, sixth of the seven Buddhas of antiquity preceding Gautama Buddha, who was the third Buddha of the five of the present age (or *kalpa*), who was born in Lumbini.

Pashupatinath

Pashupatinath, one of the most sacred destinations in
the Hindu world and the goal of countless pilgrims and
sadhus, is the most important Hindu religious site in
Nepal, whose national deity is Lord Shree Pashupatinath,
an avatar of Shiva. Always thronged with pilgrims, it is
also a UNESCO World Heritage site. Its origins predate
even the oldest of the beautiful and ancient structures
of mandirs, ashrams, pagodas, and *stupas* of the temple
complex on the banks of the Bagmati River, which started
to be developed in the fifth century under the Licchchavi
monarch Prachanda Dev.

There are many legends concerning its origin,
including the Licchchavi legend, the Devalaya legend, and
the Cow legend. According to the last, in ancient times the
current location was largely forested and a place of great
beauty, so much so that Shiva and his consort Parvati
lingered there, transforming themselves into deer. Thus
the name of Shiva became, for this episode in his life, Lord
Pashupatinath ("Lord of all animals"). The specific site of
Pashupatinath is said to result from the discovery many
centuries later of one of his antlers, broken off when he
was a deer, and revered as a *lingam*.

Swayambunath

Climb the steps to this Buddhist *stupa* in the evening for
a view over the entire Kathmandu valley. Swayambunath
is associated with Vajrayana Buddhism, followed by the
Newari people of Nepal in whose culture Swayambunath
plays a major part. It is a stunning location on a hill on
the western edge of the Kathmandu valley, and consists of

a set of temples, shrines (parts of which date back to the Licchchavi period), and of course the *stupa* itself with its iconic set of Buddha's eyes and nose, which is in fact the character in the Devanagari script for the number "One."

Seeing the Himalayan Skyline at Dawn

To be next to the "roof of the world" and not take a look at the mountains as the sun rises would be something to regret forever. Nagarkot, Dhulikhel, and Daman offer exceptional platforms for viewing the peaks of the Himalayan range of eastern Nepal.

Trekking

You can stay in idyllic villages and towns in remote locations that form the bases for trekking in some of the most beautiful landscapes in the world. The Nepal Tourism Board (NTB) Web site is a first point of contact for planning treks, and after this you can go online to research hotels/accommodation and tour guides.

Chitwan

Don't miss an elephant safari in Chitwan National Park—the ideal way to go tiger- and rhino-spotting. Details are provided on pages 146-7.

Festivals

Nepal has more festivals—local, nationwide, secular, religious, and ethnically specific—than days in the year, and there are many opportunities to see and, if you are lucky, participate in festivals taking place during your visit (see Chapter 3).

CHAPTER EIGHT

BUSINESS BRIEFING

The Business Environment

Since the 2015 Constitution Nepal's business and trade environment has been transformed. Economic liberalization has accelerated and the war on red-tape is increasingly effective. As a result growing numbers of Asian and Western businesses have come to and been thriving in Nepal. For overseas investors, technology providers, and perceptive foreign governments the opportunities being created in Nepal today are as exceptional as its current economic growth rate.

There is growth and development in renewable energy technology (hydropower), agriculture and related sectors (especially medicinal and herbal), clothing, arts and crafts, specific kinds of tourism and travel, healthcare, pharmaceuticals, security equipment and services, and education (especially vocational qualifications and IT).

Interested foreign investors should first contact their own country's overseas/international trade department about its trade and business regulations and opportunities with Nepal, including export/import taxes and tariffs (the UK for example has a zero tariff on imports from Nepal), and the trade and business section of the Nepali embassy or consulate in their country.

It is then highly advisable to conduct careful "on the ground" research, and to find appropriate trustworthy Nepali business partners. You should allow two to three visits to Nepal of not less than a week each for this.

BUSINESS CULTURE

Personal relationships are the key to business deals in Nepal. Your initial contact may well be made through business associates or common acquaintances. As nothing much gets done without the help of contacts, try to establish personal connections with as many people as possible, but be selective and do your prior research.

Business cards are important. They can be printed in English and should clearly state your position and any other credentials. Always present your card to new contacts in meetings who you feel are potential business partners. In Nepal, it is rare in business circles for people you are introduced to in formal settings not to have their own business cards.

Initially relations may be very formal. Thereafter it is sincerity, cordiality, and a personal approach that will build up the necessary level of mutual respect and trust. A business relationship will rarely be built up over the phone—Nepalis want to know exactly who they are dealing with. Socializing thus plays an important role.

Entertaining may be one way of getting yourself an audience, although some high-caste Hindus may not visit restaurants for reasons of purity (they cannot eat food prepared by lower-caste people). You may be invited to people's homes. Dinner will be seen as an opportunity to continue discussions, as well as to get to know you. This takes time, and you should not hurry it.

Fatalism may lead to an attitude to business that can on occasion be downright lackadaisical. Success is good *karma*, failure bad *karma*. The belief in cycles means that opportunities missed this time may well come around again. You may also find a reliance on superstition rather than rational planning: astrology may be used to determine "auspicious days" for meetings or the conclusion of a contract.

Another key attitude that comes across in business relations is the Nepali respect for their elders. Older participants in meetings will be treated with politeness and deference. It is also reflected in forms of address. It is polite to say *Namascar* instead of *Namaste* to an older person. If addressing people by name, you should add the *-jee* suffix as a mark of respect.

Status and Hierarchy

Most businesses in Nepal are still, to a greater or lesser degree, hierarchical. Even mundane decisions may have to go through several levels, and ultimately, it is the patriarch who decides. This can make for very slow decision-making. The *hakim's* (boss's) word is law. There is no formal review or consultation process. Staff will respect his authority unless it is perceived to be unjust.

Connections

Traditionally family connection, name, caste, and political affiliation all play a role in whether someone is given employment. This is changing with increasing levels of education, but family contacts can still be extremely important. Good relationships with clients or partners will open up new partnerships through their family ties and *aphno manche* connections.

Business Dress

Nepalis dress formally in office situations. For meetings always err on the side of formality and conservatism. Suits are the norm. Shorts are unacceptable, nor should you wear jeans. You may dispense with the tie in most situations, but a smart shirt with a collar is essential. Short sleeves are generally acceptable. Nepalese businessmen often wear Western dress, whereas women wear traditional saris or a *kurta suruval*. Western women should dress smartly and modestly. Short skirts should be avoided, and shoulders covered.

Women in Business

Greater access to education in recent years has meant that there are growing numbers of economically active women in Nepal. This is slowly improving their status as they contribute to the family income. Nepal's society until recently seemed quite male chauvinist by Western standards, and Nepali men used to deferential women may be uncomfortable dealing with forthright Western women in positions of authority. Conversely, at the end of the second decade of the twenty-first century, Western businesspeople will soon become aware that banks and major private enterprises in Nepal have women at the helm—a sign of the seismic changes in gender equality, at least in business, in Nepal.

There are businesses run by women, and various development projects aim to empower women. Earnings and increased status are liberating and many women are highly motivated.

Y. KUMARI K.
SECRETARY
MINISTRY OF INDUSTRY, COMMERCE AND SUPPLY, NEPAL

Yam Kumari Khatiwasa, Secretary at the Ministry of Commerce and Supplies.

However, social attitudes may still force women to give up work upon marriage (they need their husband's permission to work), they may be obliged to bring their baby to work with them (leaving it in a bundle on the floor somewhere while they work), and they may be expected to disappear from the workplace "to cook for a visiting brother-in-law."

Business Hours

Office hours in the Kathmandu valley are generally 9:00 a.m. until 5:00 p.m. (9:00 a.m. to 4:00 p.m. in winter), Monday to Friday. Outside the valley people

work a six-day week, with Saturday as the only day of
rest. Here offices open at 10:00 a.m. Shops are open
much longer.

MEETINGS

Making Appointments
It is probably best to make appointments by telephone,
especially when meeting for the first time, although
e-mail is increasingly used. Make appointments well
in advance and, especially outside the capital, allow for
Nepali road conditions to give yourself time to get to
the venue punctually. Be aware of Nepali eating habits,
too: an appointment before 10:00 a.m. may not be
convenient.

As decisions are generally made at the top, it is
advisable to make your approach at this level. In
internationally active organizations, secretaries will
probably speak some English. It may be a good idea to
prepare some phrases in Nepali. Exchanging courtesies
with staff will dispose them positively toward you and
increase your chances of being passed on to the boss.
Alternatively, ask a Nepali speaker to be on hand to help.

At the Meeting
Punctuality is important, although you should not be
surprised if you are kept waiting. It may also take a while
to get down to business. First meetings are likely to entail
a combination of ceremony and cordiality. Wait to be
invited to take a seat. For an initial visit this will probably

be on a sofa in a reception room or the boss's office. Do not be surprised, however, if you are invited to sit on a cushion on the floor—this is the traditional way. You will probably be offered tea, which will be brought by a *didi*, quite likely summoned by a bell. Time at the beginning is given to small talk.

When you walk into a room, you should greet everyone with a *Namaste*. Whether you shake hands with other participants in the meeting will depend on how many of them there are, and who they are. The greater the degree of exposure to Western influence, the more likely people are to expect to shake hands. It is not always appropriate to shake hands with women, and if you are talking to the representatives of rural communities, it will not be expected either. It is probably just as well to wait and see if you are offered a hand. *Namaste* should be answered with *Namaste*.

This is a very verbal culture: there may be an official agenda for the meeting, and there may be a scribe producing minutes, but the emphasis is not on paperwork. Staff memos are not typical. Decisions are pronounced verbally. People sit down together and solve problems by talking.

In urban areas English is widely spoken and understood, but discussions in Nepali may occur between Nepalis (including, of course, between your representative and those you are interested to work with) within a meeting. Sometimes understanding Nepali-English can present a problem, and you may need to ask people politely to repeat themselves. Be aware, however, that in some situations, ad hoc (nonprofessional) interpreters may only translate what they *think* you want to hear. For, example, in a non-business or charity context, the local representative of a charity may exaggerate the woes of someone who stands to benefit from a donation, or the potential benefit of that donation. Try to engage an independent translator. Students are often delighted to assist.

Business cards printed in English are likely to be exchanged at the end of meetings. Nepalis also set great store by academic titles and qualifications. These are stated on cards and it will do no harm to admire them.

Presentations

Common perceptions of what makes a good presentation apply in Nepal, too: it should be succinct, with effective use of visuals. Speak slowly and clearly and conclude with a summary of the main points to provide a basis for discussion. A polished presentation with graphics and special effects will impress, but the Nepalis also like detailed facts and figures. Both erudition and eloquence are highly valued (they like to use flowery language) and will bring you respect: it is important that you show your education, know-how, and experience. They need to see that your business proposal is serious, that it relates to them, and that you can back it up with strong financial and/or staffing support. Nepalis do not take kindly to being dictated to, so make sure you present your proposal as one of partnership, with advantages for both sides. Expect questions and consider suggestions. They will also want to discuss things exhaustively before coming to a decision.

NEGOTIATIONS

Haggling over price is a way of life in Nepal, so expect potential business partners to drive a hard bargain. Do not insult them by offering a price too obviously low. They will expect a compromise solution at the end of negotiations and so should you. On the one hand, they will be looking for the best deal available, and on the other they may consider there to be karmic reasons for the opportunity to arise again in the future.

Negotiations sometimes involve many people, and can be protracted. The process is not helped by the fact that the Nepalis may not say exactly what they are thinking. This is because they do not want to offend you or appear ungracious as hosts, and is all about maintaining face. An evasive answer may mean "no." "I'll try" may also mean "but I've no intention of succeeding." Such responses are an attempt to be polite.

If people have to admit they have not understood something, they lose face. This will have consequences: it is essential to give exact information and to make clear what it is you need from them. Refrain from criticizing or correcting colleagues, clients, or potential partners in the presence of others, and beware of patronizing or appearing arrogant. Emphasize common aims and rely on good relationships to make things possible. The situation can become fraught if differences are not settled, but confrontation may humiliate and ultimately alienate people. They will need time to discuss the options, to air their views, and to come to a conclusion. Take time yourself, and do not try to rush those you are negotiating with into a decision. Remember that negotiations, contracts, and business involve highly technical subjects and translation may be needed.

CONTRACTS

As we've seen, it is vital to establish a relationship of trust in business dealings, which takes time to develop and involves multiple meetings and forms of engagement. Traditionally, trust would take precedent over the written word, but this is no longer the case.

Company and commercial law in Nepal is based on English law. Contracts cover all aspects of a business agreement and are written up by a lawyer. They may be in English or Nepali. If in English they will be couched in formal, often, to modern eyes, somewhat eloquent language, and include lots of detail; be prepared for requests for modification at the drafting stage.

Although successful negotiations commonly culminated in a written contract, oral agreements had equal, and often superior, status. As Nepal has opened up to international business and trade, the importance of written contracts has grown for middle-level business when dealing with foreigners. Contracts are the norm for large companies working at an international level.

At small-business level, however, although the culture is changing, oral agreements are still very important for Nepali entrepreneurs who may seek to work with you—many will regard written contracts simply as provisional declarations of intent that can be subject to modification later. At all levels of business in Nepal it is strongly advisable to involve a trusted Nepali business colleague(s) in your initiatives and undertakings, whether written or oral.

The need for quality assurance is becoming widely accepted, and there are opportunities for foreign businessmen to help Nepali businesses reach Western standards of accreditation for their exports. To assist your Nepali business partners, at a very early stage in your collaboration make it clear that the completion and punctual delivery of products are essential and expected at an international level.

Regular communication and visits are necessary to ensure the smooth delivery of the terms of an agreement. At all times politeness, respect, and praise are important. A trusted local manager should be appointed to deal with things on the spot. Many investors make the mistake of appointing one agent for the whole country based in Kathmandu. It is difficult to vet local distributors in the absence of a local credit rating company—the financial details they provide cannot easily be substantiated. Here again, relationship-building is crucial. It is essential to see their operations first-hand. Developing contacts with Nepali banks and leading businessmen can help.

MANAGING DISAGREEMENT

If a conflict of interests does arise, avoid litigation, which can be drawn out and expensive. Basic legal procedures here are neither quick nor straightforward, although this too is changing. Prevention is better than cure. Employ a trusted local person to manage your affairs. Keep in regular contact and visit often. Remember, politeness, respect, and praise are key.

BUREAUCRACY AND OVERSEAS BUSINESS

In theory Nepal is open to foreign direct investment at both government and private sector levels. This has been the case for many years, but only in the past five years have practical changes been implemented to turn this position statement into a reality. Bureaucratic impediments are being identified, and solutions to the problems these cause put into effect.

The fact that civil servants were, until very recently, rotated every two years also tended to slow the wheels, as they were barely in position long enough to "learn the ropes." Among the impediments Nepal faced in terms of credibility with overseas partners were instances of decisions sometimes being changed retrospectively, forgotten, or not honored. With its commitment to achieve Developed Nation status by 2032 the government has been tackling the old ethos, and gradually but determinedly replacing it with the more serious attitude in which "Nepal is open for global trade and business."

There are frequent allegations of corruption on the part of officials in the distribution and extension of permits and approvals, the procurement of goods and services, and the awarding of contracts—a phenomenon rooted in the *jagir* culture of patronage and the *aphno manche* system of reciprocal favors and networking. However, day-to-day business is not overtly corrupt, and "favors"—such as financial inducements to individuals whose time and expertise can make the difference between the success or failure of a new project—are a way of maintaining useful contacts in business or of dealing with bureaucracy. Such contacts may later be called upon for assistance.

EMPLOYMENT FOR NON-NEPALIS

The employment options for overseas nationals in Nepal have changed. In the past, unless you were posted to Nepal by a development organization or worked for an international NGO, there were few opportunities for formal employment. Today, with the expansion of business opportunities more business visas are being issued. Foreign technical personnel may be employed, subject to the approval of the relevant government department. Travelers on tourist visas are not permitted to work for any organization, whether paid or voluntary. Business visas are issued to overseas investors or their representatives. Residential visas are only issued to individuals of international renown or who make a special contribution to the country.

CHAPTER NINE

COMMUNICATING

Nepali is the official language of Nepal and of the Indian state of Sikkim to its east, and is also spoken in other parts of northern India, Bhutan, and Burma. It is an Indo-Aryan language, closely related to Hindi and Sanskrit, and commonly written in Devanagari script. It is, however, just one of more than ninety languages spoken in Nepal, and the mother tongue of only 47.8 percent of the population. The language of higher education is, however, not Nepali, but English.

Regionally other languages dominate. Maithili and Bhojpuri are Indo-Aryan languages spoken in the Terai, Newar is common in the Kathmandu valley and central mid-hills, and other Sino-Tibetan languages are spoken in the north. In these areas, Nepali may be very much a second language.

Speaking Nepali

It is well worth learning some Nepali. It enables you to interact on a different level and with a wider variety of people, giving you a far greater insight into Nepali culture. It also gives Nepali people much pleasure to hear you try, as it is a demonstration of friendship, as well as showing consideration and respect!

Nepali is a phonetic, syllabic language, not tonal, and so easier to learn than many other Asian languages. It has a simple subject-object-verb structure, postpositions rather than prepositions, and a large number of pronouns that depend on gender, number, and the status of the person in question. Foreigners usually get away with the universally respectful form *tapai* for "you." Colloquial Nepali also has two simplified, nonconjugated verb forms, one for present/future and one for past tenses, which makes life easier.

Many English words have been assimilated, usually to describe things not common in Nepali culture, such as a "*taybull*" (table) or "*gilas*" (glass). Nepali use of conversational English beyond a basic level can sometimes be difficult to understand, however, even when spoken by educated people and their understanding of colloquial English may be limited.

Nepalis love eloquence and use what some visitors may regard as "flowery" language, which can lead to roundabout ways of saying things. They also like to flatter their audience, using expressions such as "honorable gentlemen" or "esteemed guests." These linguistic refinements should not be thought of as "quaint" or as indicating insincerity or superficiality.

Face-to-Face
After *Namaste*!, conversations usually, understandably, move on to a "How are you?" Once you know people,

you are expected to show interest in their families and speak about your own, as well as discuss what you do and where you live in your country—which will be reciprocated by the Nepali side.

One characteristic is the use of titles such as *Dai* (older brother) or *Bahini* (younger sister) as polite ways of addressing people who are not in fact relatives. These indicate respect and reflect age or respective status.

Nepalis do not have difficulty making eye contact with people they consider to be equals. However, subordinates do not generally raise their eyes. Men may not expect direct eye contact from women, nor should this be attempted with strangers, especially in remote rural areas.

Body Language

Body language in Nepal is no less likely to require translation than the spoken language.

- A gesture you will often see is a curious sideways rocking of the head. This indicates "OK"/ "Maybe," or a fairly noncommittal "Yes."
- Nepalis beckon with their palms downward. They count with their thumbs on the joints of their fingers—so three on each of four fingers.
- If someone throws their hands into the air, as if turning a dial clockwise with the right hand and counterclockwise with the left, they mean "What do you mean?" or "What's the problem?" not unlike the gesticulations in some Latin cultures.
- It is not unusual to see men holding hands—a mark

of platonic friendship only. Men and women do not touch in public.

- The feet and shoes are considered to be unclean. Always take your shoes off before you enter someone's house, and be careful never to point the soles of your feet at anyone as this would be regarded as degrading.
- The head is traditionally sacred, so you should never touch or pat even a child on the head. It is also extremely disrespectful to step over or pass anyone from above, which is why Nepali people will wait for you to come down a staircase before going up themselves.

BROADCAST MEDIA

Radio and TV have the edge over print media in a country with relatively low rates of literacy and inaccessible terrain. Radios are common in even the most remote mountain areas. Democracy brought an end to the monopoly of the state-owned Radio Nepal in the mid-1990s and there is now strong competition from FM stations.

As almost anywhere else in the world, television is the most popular form of home entertainment—witness the mushrooming of satellite dishes in the most unlikely locations. The emphasis is on talent shows, Hindi movies, and Nepali and Indian soap operas, but news and cultural programs, as well as talk shows, music programs, and documentaries are also shown.

The national, state-owned terrestrial TV broadcasters are Nepal Television, NTV Plus, and NTV News. Kantipur Television Network is the main terrestrial independent broadcaster. There are currently about fifty TV broadcasters in Nepal, most of which are private. Many also broadcast internationally via the Internet; others are specific to certain regions and localities in Nepal. Nepal Television and Radio Nepal broadcast some news bulletins in English. Foreign channels are available by satellite and on the Internet.

There are many FM frequency radio stations, such as Nepal FM, Radio Kathmandu, and Radio Kantipur. Many stations cover the Kathmandu valley, but there are multiple locality and region-specific stations, too, and others with national coverage that broadcast to particular population or interest groups, such as Voice of Youth and Gurkha FM. International stations include BBC Radio.

THE PRESS

The press today is free of censorship, but newspapers are available only in urban areas. Deliveries to towns outside the Kathmandu valley and in remoter locations can still be hampered by extreme weather conditions affecting air or road routes.

Gorkhapatra and *Kantipur* are Nepali-language dailies. The former is published by the government. *Budhabar* is a popular weekly, mainly associated with the left-wing Communist Party of Nepal (United Marxist-

Hot off the press. Ice cream seller reading the daily *Taja Khabar* ("Latest News").

Leninist, not the Maoists—see page 31). *Deshantar* is a weekly publication generally associated with the largest party, the centrist Nepali Congress.

English-language Publications
The Kathmandu Post and *The Himalayan Times* are daily English-language newspapers that include some international news. *The Rising Nepal* is an English-language government paper. More detailed analysis of national and international events can be found in the weekly *Nepali Times*.

An organization called Expatriate Community Services (www.ecs.com.np) offers language courses and produces a glossy monthly, *Your Guide To Living in Nepal*, aimed at the expatriate community in Kathmandu. It covers lifestyle, culture, and business in Nepal, and includes features by Nepalese writers and expatriates, as well as a calendar of upcoming events.

International publications, including *Time*, *Newsweek*, *The Economist*, *L'Express*, *Der Spiegel*, *Die Zeit*, and *El País* are on sale at Pilgrims Bookshop and elsewhere in Kathmandu.

THE TELEPHONE

It is mainly the wealthy who have landline telephones at home If you are calling from outside the Kathmandu valley it can be difficult to get through. This is because all lines out of the country go via Kathmandu. The use of cell phones, however, is universal—everyone either has a smartphone or access to one. Cell phone usage has pushed back the boundaries of connectivity with others in emergency and other situations in remote areas.

The main network providers are NCell (the largest network, though the signal can be poor in some remote areas) and NTC (Nepal Telecom's "Namaste" brand); there are other, smaller, providers too. The handsets used are mostly Samsung and Oppo (an Indian flagship brand) but there are types from all over the world, especially East Asia. To buy a Nepali SIM card you'll need to show ID and a photo, but registration can be completed in any cell phone shop. SIM card top-ups are easy to make: these cards come in various amount levels, and offer great value to international visitors.

Sometimes there can be problems with reception, including a scrambled connection in which you phone the correct cell phone number but get a completely unknown person. These incidents are diminishing, however, and usually only last a few minutes.

Nepalis may seem to have an abrupt telephone manner. They do not say their name, but launch straight into conversation. They're equally abrupt in putting the phone down—usually as soon as they fail to understand you or realize they do not know who you are. This can be seen alternatively as off-putting or simply functional.

THE INTERNET

The Internet in Nepal is dominated by social media, used as a means for both official and personal communication.

Web sites, on the other hand, have less of a presence than in the West. This is changing gradually though, particularly in the case of Nepali businesses interested in connecting with overseas markets, potential business partners, and international clients, who understand that without a basic-to-good Web site in English the opportunities for outreach are severely hampered. There are a number of good quality English-language Nepali Web sites, in the field of tourism in particular, and the phenomenon is growing as an outward-looking Nepal sees the Internet as an important means of boosting its economic presence.

THE SOCIAL MEDIA REVOLUTION

With the advent of social media a sociopolitical revolution is taking place in Nepal. Since the early 2010s the use of Facebook in particular has become widespread in all but the remotest parts of the country. This means not only that families who have become dispersed for economic or other reasons can stay connected, unimaginable a decade ago, but there are other impacts too. At a global level, members of the Nepali diaspora in distant lands, such as the Middle East or the United Kingdom, are able to stay in touch with family in Nepal, and diaspora community organizations can communicate and interact with the home country. Those working for social reform, on humanitarian initiatives, or for equality and inclusion can coordinate, mobilize online campaigns or demonstrations, and share news. This has undoubtedly been a factor in enabling and building the new Nepal.

When making friends in Nepal, it is almost unheard of not to be asked to become friends on Facebook, WhatsApp, Viber, and the like, and in many cases to join particular social media groups based on shared lifestyle, career, vocation, or social and political interests. Clearly the social media revolution is affecting almost every aspect of daily life. This is all the more extraordinary considering that before the Internet age communications between friends and distant family members, whether overseas or within the country, was very difficult. There was minimal phone contact, journeys often took more than twenty-four hours, letters could take many days to arrive, and reunions were very infrequent, perhaps just once or twice a year. Today many younger Nepalis spend hours on social media, and social and community group officers and members utilize social media posts as their prime means of mass communication. Most of the latter are in Nepali/Devanagari, but you will find that on a personal level, especially friend-to-friend, social media text messages between Nepalis quite often are in English.

MAIL

Outbound mail from Nepal is reasonably reliable from Kathmandu or Pokhara. "Snail mail" between towns within Nepal can be slower than sending things internationally, although it does seem to work eventually. Poste restante (general delivery) services are available only in Kathmandu. The main post office in Kathmandu is on Kantipath, near the stadium and New Road. You can buy stamps and hand in letters for posting at Pilgrims Bookshops in Kathmandu and Pokhara.

A faster option is a courier service—more expensive than the post but generally reliable and efficient. Couriers are of course as susceptible as any other road user to disruption caused by the weather, landslides, or strikes. You generally need to pick things up from a designated office in the town, signing for anything you receive.

CONCLUSION

King Prithvi Narayan Shah, who unified Nepal in the eighteenth century, described his country as "a flower garden of four *varnas* [castes] and thirty-six *jats* [communities]." This positive image captures the beauty and also the diversity of Nepal. Its incongruities and contrasts will inevitably surprise you. So too, despite the great disparities in wealth and education, will its social harmony, which is underpinned by an essentially religious outlook.

Whatever the reason for your visit, some knowledge of Nepali culture will enhance the experience and give you realistic expectations. Once you get to know the Nepalis, their friendliness, stoicism, warmth, and hospitality will leave a lasting impression so that when it comes to saying good-bye, the Nepali way will seem the most appropriate: "*Pheri bhetaula!*" "We'll meet again," which also means "See you later."

FURTHER READING

Bista, Dor Bahadur. *Fatalism and Development: Nepal's Struggle for Modernization*. Hyderabad: Orient Longman Pty Limited, 1999.

Chaulagain, Luna (translated by Ganesh Chaulagain and Phil Grayston). *Himalayan Folk Tales*. Nepal: locally published in 2001 and available at Pilgrims Bookshop.

Dixit, Kanak Mani, and Shastri Ramachandaran. *State of Nepal*. Lalitpur, Nepal: Himal Books, 2002.

Jha, Prashant. *Battles of the New Republic: A Contemporary History of Nepal*. New Delhi: Aleph Book Publications, 2014.

Krakauer, Jon. *Into Thin Air*. London: Pan Books, 1998.

Mayhew, Bradley, and Lindsay Brown and Paul Stiles. *Lonely Planet Nepal*. Victoria, Australia: Lonely Planet Global Ltd, 2018.

McGunnigle, Nicola. *Four Seasons In Nepal: Inside stories of hope and empowerment in a developing nation*. Mona Vale, NSW, Australia: Ark House Press, 2017.

Pemble, John. *Britain's Gurkha War: The Invasion of Nepal, 1814–16*. Barnsley, Yorkshire: Frontline Books, 2008.

Subedi, Abhi. *Nepali Theatre As I See It*. Kathmandu: Aarohan, 2006.

Subedi, Abhi, and Krishna Pradhan and Michael Hutt. *Teach Yourself Nepali*. London: Hodder & Stoughton, 1999.

Upadhyay, Samrat. *Arresting God in Kathmandu*. Kolkata: Rupa & Co, 2003.

Werner, David. *Where There Is No Doctor—A Village Health Care Handbook*. London: Macmillan Education, 1993.

Useful Web Sites

https://www.welcomenepal.com/ (Nepal Tourism Board Web site)

www.ecs.com.np (contemporary Nepali culture)

http://www.living.com.np/ (daily life in Nepal)

http://kathmandupost.ekantipur.com/category/national (online version)

http://kathmandupost.ekantipur.com/category/sports (sports information)

www.weallnepali.com (news portal)

www.creativenepal.co.uk (Nepal arts resource)

http://foodsofnepal.com/ (Nepali cuisine)

http://nepaliculturalheritage.com/ (Nepali diaspora culture)

PICTURE CREDITS

INDEX